Praise for
A Positive Plan for Creating More Fun, Less Whining

"This jam-packed creative manual is sizzling with ideas to keep a spark in your family time. Sweet is the sound of family laughter . . . memories last a lifetime . . . so have a plan!"

Patsy Clairmont
Women of Faith speaker
Author, *All Cracked Up*

"Karol offers fun-in-the-now by savoring each stage of your child's life with complete and concise tips for being the encouraging, positive, and FUN mom."

Jane Jarrell
Author of *The Frazzled Factor* and *Simple Hospitality*

a positive plan

for creating

more fun, less *whining*

KAROL LADD

W PUBLISHING GROUP
A Division of Thomas Nelson Publishers
Since 1798
www.wpublishinggroup.com

A Positive Plan for Creating More Fun, Less Whining

Published by W Publishing Group, a division of Thomas Nelson, Inc., P.O. Box 141000, Nashville, TN 37214.

Cover design: Brand Navigation
Interior design: Stacy Clark

Library of Congress Cataloging-in-Publication Data

Ladd, Karol.
    A positive plan for creating more fun, less whining / Karol Ladd.
       p. cm.
Includes bibliographical references.
    ISBN 0-8499-0711-X
    1. Family—Religious life. 2. Family recreation. I. Title.
    BV4526.3.L33 2006
    649'.5—dc22

                                                                2006005739

Printed in the United States of America

06 07 08 09 10 RRD 9 8 7 6 5 4 3 2 1

A good laugh is sunshine in a house.

WILLIAM MAKEPEACE THACKERAY

A special thanks to my precious friends who sprinkled fun ideas throughout this book: Beth R., Leslie H., Leslie C., Amy R., Karen S., Karen M., Beth D., Caroline B., Carol F., Leslie W., Liz T., Becky J., Jane J., and LaVerne D.

Contents

Step Three:
Build Fond Memories

Step Four:
Welcome Friends and Family

Pure and Simple Fun

There ain't much fun in medicine,
but there's a good deal of medicine in fun.

JOSH BILLINGS

He who has a glad heart has a continual feast.

PROVERBS 15:15 AMP

Do the words "I'm bored" strike a chord of fear and anxiety in your spirit?

Does your stress level rise when you hear a question like, "Can Steve and Tommy spend the night tonight?"

Is there tension in your neck and shoulders when one of the kids begins to whine, "This isn't fun! Can't we do something else?"

Breathe a sigh of relief; help is here.

Every person who has kids or works with kids knows the benefit of having a few fresh ideas to create more fun and less whining. Whether you are a parent, grandparent, teacher, youth worker, vacation Bible school volunteer, aunt, uncle, or neighbor, I'm guessing you would prefer to enjoy the kids around you rather than being annoyed by them. Consider this book an essential resource to keep on hand whenever those precious charges are in your care. Within the pages of this book, you will find activities for any time, any place, any occasion, and kids of any age.

Recently an elderly friend asked me, "So, Karol, what is your latest project?" I told him the name of this book, and a big smile broke across his face as he glanced at the grandchild he had cared for during the weekend. "Hurry up and write that one!" he said with a slight tone of desperation.

Even the best of kids have their trying moments. I want to equip you with fun artillery so you will be ready just in case grumbling or whining should erupt. I also want to help you get to the root of whining and plant contentment and gratitude in its place.

Fun in the Making

Fun is an important element of a child's life, yet in our hurry-up, gotta-go society we rarely seem to fit it into the schedule. Certainly, there are times when amusing moments just seem to surface out of nowhere; but for the most part, fun must be deliberately planned. I would like to offer you a positive and practical plan for creating fun and building delightful memories!

We will begin by adopting a new attitude toward fun. I want to show you simple and innovative ways to create an atmosphere that welcomes delight into your home. Next, we'll move into fresh ideas for enjoying family moments together. We will cover terrific travel tips, dinnertime delights, sanity-saving shopping tips, and beautiful ways to reach out in compassion together outside the walls of our home. The third section of the book deals specifically with creative and unique ways to build fond memories for our kids. Most of us want our kids to reflect on their childhood memories in a positive way, so in this section we will explore ways to enhance birthday celebrations as well as ways to make the most of special themes and significant occasions.

Finally, fun happens with friends, so I've devoted an entire section to creatively welcoming and enjoying friends and extended family members. You will find imaginative ideas for outdoor adventures as well as indoor ingenuity. And, of course, the book wouldn't be complete if I didn't offer survival tips for those times when the kids have friends visiting for a sleepover. Trust me, you will make it through with flying colors.

You may be wondering where I got all of the ideas for this book. Some of the ideas come from my own experiences as a camp counselor and as a teacher. I was trained in the trenches in how to rescue kids from boredom and create an experience that is meaningful and fun. I'm also a mom, so I've tested many of the parties, crafts, and games on my own family throughout the years. You will see that I've also included ideas from a tremendous repertoire of resources. In fact, you will find a list of some of my favorite resources at the end of the book. One of the best resources was my friends, who will share with you in this book their own fun activities they have experienced with their families.

Stop Whining

Perhaps you read the title of this book and thought that you could use a little less whining around the house. Now, I'm not sure if you are talking about your kids' whining or your own whining. Either way, as you increase the opportunities for smiles in your home, your kids will whine a little less often, and you will find yourself uplifted as well. Fun can't get rid of all the whining, but it can make a huge dent in it. Whining is also a heart issue, so we will get to the nitty-gritty of whining in chapter 2. (You may want to turn straight there if this is an emergency.)

It is my hope that by giving you the ideas in this book, I will be giving you a gift, a gift of joy. When my kids grow up, I want them to look back at their childhood years with fond memories.

I'm sure you feel that way too. An overabundance of grumbling and complaining would tend to muddy those wonderful memories. At the end of each chapter, you will find a wonderful way to encourage your kids' hearts and spiritual wisdom through a family devotional.

All in all, *A Positive Plan for Creating More Fun, Less Whining* is a reference book to help you create great memories. Keep it handy for when the entire neighborhood descends on your backyard or when you are planning that next vacation or putting together another birthday party. Fun doesn't have to be difficult or costly. It begins with a willing heart and develops through a positive plan. Even the most uncreative, unresourceful type of person can do it. Making wonderful memories is easier than you think!

1

Laughter: The Perfect Glue for Family Bonding

Genuine laughing is the vent of the soul, the nostrils of the heart, and it is just as necessary for health and happiness as spring water is for a trout.

JOSH BILLINGS

A cheerful heart is good medicine,
but a crushed spirit dries up the bones.

PROVERBS 17:22

When is the last time you had a good, hearty laugh? Really, honestly, take a moment to think about it. Hopefully you don't have to think back too far. Sometimes just the memory of a gut-wrenching guffaw starts me laughing all over again. (I had to stop writing several times during this paragraph just to regain my composure.)

Without a doubt, a good dose of humor levels some of the bumps in life and lightens the load of our day-to-day routine. Victor Hugo said, "Laughter is the sun that drives winter from the human face."[1] I'd add that laughter is the sunshine that melts the winter frost that sometimes settles on human relationships.

We need to laugh more often with family and friends. Not

1

only is it good for our health; it's good for our life. Perhaps you are thinking, *But I don't feel like laughing. My life is the pits right now.* I want to invite you to take a short mental vacation from the pit you are in and travel to a place of heartfelt joy. You will find that as you fill your heart and mind with cheer, your perspective may change on the challenges you face.

Now, I don't want to gloss over the fact that there are times in our lives when we must grieve and cry. As Solomon said, "There is a time for everything, and a season for every activity under heaven . . . a time to weep and a time to laugh, a time to mourn and a time to dance" (Ecclesiastes 3:1, 4). Realistically, there are certain times in all of our lives when we must work through the pain of loss or hurt or grief. Please don't get me wrong. I'm not diminishing the importance of those times, but I am saying that there are many opportunities for delight and laughter as well. And sometimes humor may be the God-given salve that helps soothe the hurt and heal the pain.

Superglue

Humor can be sticky. By that, I mean that laughing together can bring family members closer and create a unique bonding by smoothing over some of the prickly edges. In his book *The Laughter Prescription*, Dr. Laurence Peter says humor serves an important role in easing tensions, both in the individual and in relationships with others. "Laughter provides the outlet for otherwise unacceptable feelings, behaviors and impulses by facilitating talking about or acting out conflicts and emotions in a safe, nonthreatening way."[2]

My dear friend Beth, mother of four, can attest to the blessing of laughter. When her youngest son was a curious toddler, he happened to find several paint bottles on the kitchen table. Being the industrious toddler that he was, he wanted to paint with his newfound treasure. Unfortunately, there were no paintbrushes to help him out; but who needs paintbrushes when you have open bottles of paint? Little Kyle took a bottle in each hand. While holding them upside down, he walked through the beautifully carpeted family room, then the dining room, and was about to enter the kitchen when he met up with Beth.

She will never forget this poignant moment of decision. Here she stood, looking at her proud toddler with nearly empty paint bottles and her newly decorated carpet. At this point she could have screamed bloody murder or she could have stayed quiet, calm, cool, and collected. Neither of these options worked for her. Instead, she began to laugh hysterically. The humor of the moment had hit her like a wave of cool, fresh water. She knew her son had not done this out of direct disobedience or defiance. It was simply childhood foolishness. Yes, he needed to learn not to do it again, and that would come in a moment.

Wise Beth chose to make this a fond family memory. You can be sure that either way it would have been a memory, but Beth chose a fond memory through laughter instead of a horrible memory through screaming. She gathered the family together for a good laugh. They took pictures, and then they all worked together to clean up the mess. The sibling who left the paint bottles out had double duty, I'm sure. Kyle's paint incident happened almost twenty years ago, but the family still laughs about it to this day— thanks to Beth's ability to see the lighter side of life.

Certainly we can't laugh at every wrong thing our kids do. We shouldn't make them think that it's OK or funny to make a mess or act irresponsibly. Handle laughter with wisdom, but don't miss opportunities to allow laughter to build your family memories and bond you in the process.

The Laugh Cure

Humor helps keep family challenges and unforeseen circumstances in perspective, and it can prevent our stress levels from rising out of control. Yes, humor can have a healing effect both emotionally and physically. A number of years ago, Norman Cousins, the famous editor of the *Saturday Review,* was told he had a severe case of an incurable, progressive, connective tissue disease. He decided that instead of sitting around and allowing the pain to take over, he would become proactive in his health-care management and especially in his attitude. One of the things he decided to do was to obtain copies of old television shows and movies he had always enjoyed, such as *Candid Camera* and Marx Brothers films. He also decided to read humorous books. He reported that ten minutes of genuine belly laughter would relieve his intense pain for hours.

While Norman was in the hospital, he started a routine of watching movies, laughing, sleeping, watching movies, laughing, sleeping, and so on. After a while, he was moved out of the hospital because his laughter was disturbing other patients, but he continued his treatment with astounding results. Using massive doses of vitamin C and a tremendous amount of laughter every day, he experienced a gradual withdrawal of his symptoms and eventually regained most of his freedom of movement. You can read his entire story in his book, *Anatomy of an Illness.*[3]

When former actress Lisa Whelchel became a stay-at-home mom with three young children, she invited a handful of friends to gather at her home once a week to play games and enjoy some good ol' mom time together. The women found that the time of laughter and fellowship was therapeutic and provided a good dose of encouragement. They began affectionately calling their gathering "The Good Medicine Club," because their laughter together changed their attitudes and helped them through some of the challenges of motherhood in a positive way. Lisa carries on the tradition today with her MomTime clubs and events.[4]

Be Jovial

If we took an official Laugh-O-Meter around the world to detect the source of most of the earth's laughter, sadly, I'm not sure we would find the highest meter reading in Christian homes and churches. Yet Christian families ought to be among the most joyful people on earth. Why? Not because we have fewer problems, but because we have a God who loves us and is with us through the difficulties. We have a wonderful heavenly Father, who has allowed us to partake in his wonderful grace through his Son, Jesus. He invites us to cast our cares and needs on him. He gives us hope and peace and forgiveness.

> In fact, Paul implored the early Christians, "Rejoice in the Lord always. Again I will say, rejoice!" (Philippians 4:4 NKJV). Certainly there are times to grieve and cry, but let's not miss the wonderful opportunities to experience joy. In his book *Lighten Up!* humorist Ken Davis says, "The world is desperate for any sign of joy. Men and women have searched the realms of materialism, hedonism, and even religion looking for joy. They've even peeked into churches. They've studied the faces of those who claim to know the author of joy —and found nothing joyful at all. Churches ought to be filled not only with the sound of solemn prayers and practical lessons from God's Word; laughter too should be heard bouncing from the walls."[5]

Good, Clean Laughter

Let's be careful to keep our laughter in the right context. As the philosopher Johann Wolfgang von Goethe wisely noted, "Men show their character in nothing more clearly than by what they think laughable." Fun and amusement should not come at the expense of another. We must guard ourselves carefully from trying to get a laugh or a rise out of people by putting another person down. Sarcasm can often hurt another and dismantle someone's self-esteem. Laughter at the expense of another is not funny at all.

So how do you generate good, hearty, belly-busting guffaws, even when you may not feel like it? Consider some of the following:

- Visit clean joke sites on the Internet, such as www.ahajokes.com, www.cleanfunnyjoke.com, or www.tickleu.com.
- Sign up to receive daily jokes from sites such as www.clean-joke-of-the-day.com.
- Watch good, clean movies that make you laugh.
- Play fun games together.
- Keep a joke book or riddle book in the car or by the dinner table so you will have it readily available.
- Read books with humorous stories, jokes, or cartoons.
- Rent a video of sports or commercial bloopers.
- Get together with a hilarious friend.
- Watch videos of stand-up comedians, such as Anita Renfroe or Chonda Pierce.
- Create a humor survival kit complete with joke books, squeaky toys, funny games, hilarious pictures and cartoons, and funny shows on DVD.
- Do the activities from a fun, innovative, brilliantly creative book (wow, one comes to mind immediately— *A Positive Plan for Creating More Fun, Less Whining*!).

Seriously, good, hearty laughter is easy to come by. It may take a small amount of deliberate effort, but the payoff is worth it. Having fun together as a family increases your probability of chuckles and hopefully will lead to a full-blown explosion of hilarity.

It's easy to think that life's too busy or serious to take time for fun and laughter, but the truth is that life is too short not to. More important, our family life is enriched and strengthened through the smiles and laughter we share together. Let's make a decision to move in a positive direction by providing more opportunities for laughter with our kids.

Family Fun Devotional

Read: Proverbs 15:13; Philippians 4:4

Talk:

- Why do you think God created laughter?
- What is one of your favorite funny memories that you have enjoyed as a family?
- What are some reasons that Christians have to rejoice?

Do:

Do a family joke search. Tell everyone they have twenty minutes to find a funny joke to read or tell to the family. It would be a good idea to have some joke books available. (I get most of mine from a half-price bookstore.) They can also go online to a clean joke Web site. You may need to help young ones find theirs. Return to the kitchen table in twenty minutes and allow everyone to present their jokes. Vote on whose joke is the funniest. You may want to videotape your family comedy hour for future viewing and laughter.

2

How to Raise a Whiner

Happiness is inward, and not outward; and so, it does not depend on what we have, but on what we are.

HENRY VAN DYKE

In everything you do, stay away from complaining and arguing, so that no one can speak a word of blame against you.

PHILIPPIANS 2:14–15 TLB

So far, I haven't met any parents who actually want their kids to be whiners. Very few people intentionally invite the annoying sounds of "I want . . ." or the irritating complaint of "Why do I have to?"

So how does it happen? How do well-meaning parents gradually find themselves with sniveling, whining, negative kids? It's really quite simple. The truth is that whining comes naturally to us all; we rarely need formal training to add it to our attitude arsenal. On the other hand, it takes determination to raise content kids.

In a way, whining is like the weeds in our garden. We don't plant them or particularly want them there, but like it or not, they will overtake our garden if we let them. If our intention is to have a beautiful garden, then we must guard against nurturing the weeds. Instead of allowing them to grow, we need to pull the weeds and plant something beautiful in their place. Since the weeds of whining pop up in our kids without much effort, we don't want to encourage their growth. On the other hand, we need to plant seeds of joy, gratitude, and peace that will take root and grow into healthy, happy adults.

By taking the negative-example approach of "how to raise a whiner," I hope to help each of us as parents recognize some of the possible ways we inadvertently allow grumbling and complaining to grow in our children. Perhaps you are saying to yourself, "Not me; I don't encourage whining." Trust me, I said the same thing. Then I ate my words as I began to write this chapter and to see myself in some of these scenarios (I'm embarrassed to admit).

The tough truth is that whining kids grow into whining adults. It is not only in your family's best interest but in the interest of society at large that you weed the whining from your family garden. Your friends and extended family will be grateful. And of course your kids' future spouses will thank you too!

Here's a tongue-in-cheek look at how to grow a strong grumbler. Don't worry; we'll look at how to plant seeds of contentment in the second half of the chapter.

Lesson One: Give In to the Whining

You've had a hard day, and you just don't want to hear it anymore. It certainly is easier to give in to your child's nagging than to say no to him and deal with his crying and screaming. So go ahead. Give in. Give him what he wants. It will make it easier for you to give in the next time he whines for something, and that time is probably just around the corner.

Careful now. If in a weak moment you decide to tell your kids "no" or "wait your turn," they may learn qualities such as patience and self-discipline. If your goal is to raise a whiner, those positive qualities will never do. Immediate gratification and giving in to desires are what you are after. Your best strategy for raising a whiner is to reason with your little grumbler and eventually give in. It will fortify his resolve to continue his demands, and it will help him develop stronger negotiation and manipulation techniques.

Lesson Two: Scream Back at Them

"Stop it! I don't want to hear another word! Just be quiet!"

Now your child knows she has your attention! And that's just what she wanted—your attention. As you scream, your child will temporarily stop whining and you can feel great about weed-whacking the problem, even though the roots of whining are still there. The good news is you have taught your kids two indelible lessons in the process.

First, you have shown them that screaming is a very powerful tool. There's a good chance they will follow your example and use the power of a scream the next time they want something.

Second, the loud attention you give to whining teaches your kids a solid way to get your attention. Mind you, they don't consciously plan this out, and they don't necessarily enjoy your loud screaming, but the next time they feel they need your attention, they know just how to get it. Whine, whine, whine—and boy, do you give them your full attention!

Lesson Three: Grumble and Complain About Your Problems

As we mentioned in the previous lesson, kids learn best if they can watch your own example, so if you really want a bumper crop of complainers, you will need to complain on a regular basis. You know the old routine: "This restaurant never gets my food right." "The music at church is too loud." "The coach doesn't rotate the players enough." "The neighbors won't keep their yard clean." "The school isn't training its teachers properly." "No one is ever sensitive to my feelings." "If only this or that."

It's pretty standard procedure for most of us. Be sure your kids don't hear you express thankfulness for anything, or they may learn gratitude (a definite disadvantage for a whiner). And be very careful that your kids do not pick up on the times when you choose to look at the good in a situation. Then they may begin overlooking negatives and seeking out the positives in a circumstance or a person. By all means, don't let the kids focus on the positives, or they may miss the negative stuff altogether.

Lesson Four: Shield Them from Difficulties and Pain

Guard your kids carefully so that they never get a difficult teacher or lose a tryout or have a coach who won't play them on the A team. If your children begin to feel any sort of disappointment or pain, pacify them immediately by buying them something or blaming it on someone else. If you really want to go the extra mile, yell at the coach or spread rumors about how bad the teacher is and try to get your precious angel moved to another class.

Pain and challenges in a child's life may lead to qualities such as strength, perseverance, and compassion toward others, which are certainly qualities that are unbecoming of a whiner. Your child deserves the best, and you make sure you give it to him. That old adage about learning lessons through the hard knocks of life is a crock (at least you keep telling yourself that). Getting one's own way without any challenges or difficulties teaches much more valuable lessons, such as the "me first" and "I deserve" attitudes.

Lesson Five: Blame Others

"It's OK; it's not your fault." This age-old concept helps our kids advance to a higher level of complaint and moves them into the category of "I couldn't possibly be wrong." Fortunately, the blame game allows them to get away with just about anything they want. For example, an outburst of anger at the restaurant isn't little Ashley's fault; it was the waitress's fault because she didn't bring out the right flavor of ice cream. Or Sammy grabbed the toy out of the other little boy's hands, but it was because the other kid wouldn't share it with him.

Blaming others offers a child an entitlement to whining and delivers it on a silver platter with his or her name engraved on it. The mere hint of personal responsibility begins to strike at the very core of complaining. Keep that self-centeredness intact in your kids by steering clear of any sort of self-discipline or self-sacrifice. Forgiveness and understanding of other people's faults are out of the question and would only lead to your child's showing kindness or compassion.

Planting Good Seeds

Obviously, we would prefer to steer clear of the five ways to raise a whiner! Instead, let's equip ourselves with the tools we need to create a beautiful crop of contentment. If we are going to be intentional about raising content kids, we need the proper tools not only to weed out the whining but to till the soil and then plant good seeds. Let's consider several ways to counterattack the weeds of whining with the beautiful flowers of contentment and gratitude.

One of the most important tools to help us dig out the roots of whining is discipline. When we are wise about disciplining our kids, we do not breed rebellion. Instead, we begin to develop a confident obedience in our children. This is not a book on discipline (although I do recommend my favorite ones in the reference section in the back), yet discipline plays a vital part in curbing whining.

Wisdom in what we say, consistency in what we do, and teaching to the heart of the issue lead to effective discipline. The integrity of our word is vital. Our "no" must mean "no," just as our "yes" must mean "yes." If we say, "No, you may not have that candy bar," but then it turns into "maybe" and eventually "OK, go ahead," we teach our kids that if they persist in their whining long enough, we can be worn down. On the other hand, if we say we are going to do something and then follow through to the best of our ability, we teach our kids that we mean what we say. We must be wise in what we say we are going to do and then to the best of our ability follow through with it.

Other tools that help us plant good seeds are the example by which we live, a heart of understanding, and the lessons we impart. Our example speaks volumes. Yes, our kids learn how to act and live as they watch our lives in action. If we want grateful, content kids, they need to see these character qualities being played out in our own lives. They need to hear us thank God for his provision, even in challenges. They need to see us reaching out in compassion to others instead of thinking only of ourselves.

A heart of understanding helps us to effectively teach and discipline our kids instead of exasperating them. We need to examine the child, recognizing that each child is a unique creation of God. A wise teacher recognizes different learning styles and teaches to the heart of the student. We must be deliberate about teaching our kids the fear of the Lord and strong moral values. These lessons may happen over dinnertime or during a family devotional time. Lessons can emerge as you spend time together on a family trip or running errands. Sometimes we teach lessons through a planned time, and other times those lessons surface through teachable moments.

The tools of sound discipline, good examples, and wise lessons prepare the soil of our children's hearts and create fertile soil for us to plant positive qualities. What are those good seeds we want to plant in place of the weeds of whining? Here are a few that will keep complaining at a minimum.

Flexibility. Plans change, situations don't always turn out as we hoped they would, and people fail; therefore, one of the most important lessons our kids can learn is to adjust without complaint. Now, this is hard for some of us adults, yet it is a life lesson we need to teach our kids early on so they can learn to roll with the punches rather than complain about them.

Compassion. Grumbling and whining seem to dwindle as we get our eyes off of ourselves and onto the needs of others. When we care for others and reach out in love, we no longer see our own little problems in the same light. Chapter 10 in this book offers fun and creative ways to reach out and bless others in need.

Forgiveness. The Lord's Prayer says, "Forgive us our sins, just as we have forgiven those who have sinned against us" (Matthew 6:12 NLT). The apostle Paul also reminds us, "Make allowance for each other's faults and forgive the person who offends you. Remember, the Lord forgave you, so you must forgive others" (Colossians 3:13 NLT). As we recognize our own sinfulness, we know the importance of forgiving others. We are all sinners, we all make mistakes, and we all need forgiveness. As we realize the grace that has been extended toward us through Christ, we can't help but have grace toward other people.

Thankfulness. Gratitude is a surefire way to diminish our worry and complaints about what we don't have. Teaching our kids gratitude is a valuable life lesson. They can hear and learn thankfulness from us each day as we say, "I'm so thankful for . . ." We can encourage thankfulness around the dinner table as we say grace and thank the Lord specifically for his blessings. As soon as our kids are able to write, we want to teach them the importance of writing thank-you notes. And each night as our kids go to bed, let's review some of the things we can thank God for that day.

I love the idea my friend Liz uses with her kids. She told me, "When my kids whine, I usually break into song. I sing all the time to my kids, real songs as well as goofy ones. When they whine, I sing 'Count Your Blessings,' and then I have them name ten blessings they can think of. They absolutely hate this and roll their eyes and even warn the younger siblings about what will happen if they complain. Sometimes I have to admit that I enjoy the torture a little. But I feel like the bottom line is they laugh a little, and maybe in some simple way, they consider the good things they should be thankful for."

Contentment. Our contentment is not based on the things we have or even the people in our lives. Contentment is a heart issue. We can teach our kids at an early age the difference between needs and wants by helping them identify the two. If you hear your daughter say, "I need . . . ," talk to her about it and discuss the necessity of the item and whether it is something she actually needs or simply wants. It's OK to get our wants sometimes, but it is important to know the difference.

In Philippians 4:11–13, the apostle Paul addresses the issue of contentment and tells us the key to having a content heart: "I have learned to be content in whatever circumstances I am. I know how to get along with humble means, and I also know how to live in prosperity; in any and every circumstance I have learned the secret of being filled and going hungry, both of having abundance and suffering need. I can do all things through Him who strengthens me" (NASB).

We may not have the strength to be content in our own power, but we can be content through Christ, who gives us strength. What a powerful lesson to teach our kids! Turn your eyes toward the Lord when you feel an urge to grumble or be discontent. Ask the Lord to give you his strength to be content no matter what the circumstances.

The Proper Place for Complaints

It is fair to say that there are honestly times when we need to respectfully submit a complaint or request. This can be done without whining or grumbling, and it is important that we give our kids the tools to make a valid request. Here are a few important points to teach your children when it comes to presenting a complaint. Knowing how to do this will not only help them to work past the whines but also help them in the future. As adults, in most areas of employment, they will need to know how to submit a request and/or present their case.

Consider your timing. Timing is everything. It is not wise to approach people with a complaint if they are busy, tired, or frustrated. Set an appointment to discuss the issue (yes, even with family members) when you know you will have their full attention.

Show respect. Speak with respect and show respect for the other person's judgment. Don't be emotional or argumentative, and don't put the other person down.

Begin with a positive. Provide a sincere positive opening statement. Compliment or thank them. Tell them you understand why they have made the rule that they have made. "I understand why you have set the curfew at eleven o'clock, because I know you love me and care about my safety, and I thank you for that."

State your case clearly. Tell them kindly and clearly why you are approaching them. "I am here to ask you to consider changing my curfew for this weekend."

Present a logical alternative. Give them an idea of what you would like. "Could we possibly extend my curfew to twelve thirty just for this weekend?"

Give one or two valid reasons. You need to let them know in very reasonable terms why you are making the request. "It's homecoming weekend, and the dance isn't over until midnight, and I need to take my date home."

Restate your request. Make it short and to the point. "So I'm asking for an extended curfew until twelve thirty for this weekend, and I will respect your decision."

Then stay quiet. Give them time to consider your request and respect the decision. The way you handle this request will make a difference in their response to future requests.

Parents, if your child has a reasonable request and submits it in a respectful way, try if at all possible to say yes or make a healthy compromise. It is our job not to major on the minor stuff. If our kids have learned to be respectful and thoughtful in their requesting (not whining and not fake), then we need to encourage them.

Everything Doesn't Taste Like Chocolate Cake

My friend Leslie has a funny saying when it comes to whining and tough times. It began when her daughter Amanda wouldn't eat her vegetables, but she loved chocolate cake. "Why do I have to eat my vegetables?" Amanda would complain. Finally, in exasperation Leslie said, "Amanda, every food can't taste like chocolate cake!" The saying stuck, and now the Hodge family uses the phrase as a reminder that sometimes life is hard. It can't always be fun and games.

I hope that through this chapter you have seen the importance of teaching our kids that we are not going to enjoy and love every part of our day, but through God's strength we can become content in our circumstances. We can't simply weed-whack whining with yelling and screaming, nor can we weed-whack it by trying to make life fun, fun, fun. We must pull whining up by the roots. The roots of self-centeredness, discontent, and selfish pride can be found in each one of us.

There is only one real solution. When Christ becomes the center of our lives, our hearts and minds change their focus. We begin to see things with a heavenly perspective, allowing us to be grace-filled, forgiving, and flexible. We also love and serve others as we follow Christ's example. We can't change our core, but God can through the power of his Holy Spirit.

Jesus reminds us that God is the gardener who tends us and prunes us and produces beautiful, loving fruit in our lives. Listen to his words:

> "I am the true vine, and my Father is the gardener. He cuts off every branch that doesn't produce fruit, and he prunes the branches that do bear fruit so they will produce even more. You have already been pruned for greater fruitfulness by the message I have given you. Remain in me, and I will remain in you. For a branch cannot produce fruit if it is severed from the vine, and you cannot be fruitful apart from me.
>
> "Yes, I am the vine; you are the branches. Those who remain in me, and I in them, will produce much fruit. For apart from me you can do nothing." (John 15:1–5 NLT)

Ultimately, our weakness brings us to our need for him, and that's a good place to be. May the Lord help each of us to grow in flexibility, compassion, grace, thankfulness, and contentment as he weeds out grumbling and discontentment from our hearts.

Family Fun Devotional

Read: Philippians 2:14–15

Talk:

- Why do you think people complain or grumble?
- Do you think people are happier or sadder when they complain?
- What is the opposite of grumbling?

Do:

Weed and Plant

Weed: If possible, locate some weeds that you are able to eliminate in your yard. As a family, talk about how it doesn't work to just pull off the top of the weeds. Use tools to get down to the roots and weed a few together. Point out that just as weeds grow quickly and easily, so whining and complaining easily grow in our attitudes. For older children, talk about some of the roots of whining (discontent, self-centeredness, bitterness). Talk together about how the Lord is able to weed those things out of our hearts and make us new creations.

Plant: Now plant some seeds together in your garden or in a pot. Talk about the fact that when we plant the seeds of God's truth in our hearts and minds and allow God's Spirit to water them, our attitudes grow into beautiful plants with the fruit of love, joy, peace, patience, kindness, goodness, faithfulness, gentleness, and self-control.

step
one

Adopt a New Attitude

Your attitude is a powerful tool for positive action. It's inherently interwoven into everything you do.

KEITH HARRELL

Always be full of joy in the Lord. I say it again—rejoice!
THE APOSTLE PAUL, FROM PRISON (PHILIPPIANS 4:4 NLT)

Joy is waiting to be discovered all around us. We must open our hearts and minds to being joyful people.

3

Being Fun

Do you remember the "fun mom" in your neighborhood during your growing-up years? You know, the mom who always welcomed you into her home with a smile. She usually had something for you to eat or drink, and she wasn't worried if the house looked perfect or not. She may have been your own mom, greeting your friends with open arms, or she could have been your best friend's mom, or a mom down the street, or even a Sunday school teacher. Whoever she was, you knew she was special because she welcomed life and laughter into her home.

I'm guessing that the "fun house" in the neighborhood wasn't necessarily the biggest and the best house with the most incredible and unbelievable stuff. Expensive toys, games, and equipment don't always translate into unabashed fun. Often it is the simplicity of enjoying each other and having a wonderful time creating great moments together that erupts into pure and frivolous fun. That's because fun begins with an attitude, not things. If you decide you are going to enjoy life, generally speaking, you will! And if you look for fun, you will find it.

Perhaps you have thought, *I'd love to be the fun mom, but that's just not me.* I want to say that you (yes, even you) can have an open heart to fun and laughter. It's a choice. Our attitude toward life is a choice. Joy-filled fun is all around us. We can either look for it and welcome it with open arms or close our hearts to it and worry about the mess. Some people even choose to shun fun and laughter because they would rather wallow in their current troubles or bitterness from the past or worries for the future.

Fun in the Now

If you sit around and wait for a fun mood or the feeling of happiness, you may be sitting for a long time. We can discover joy all around us right now if we will merely open our eyes to it. Fun begins by having a new perspective, not necessarily new circumstances. Paul encouraged the early Christians to "pray continually; give thanks in all circumstances, for this is God's will for you in Christ Jesus" (1 Thessalonians 5:17–18). He wasn't telling Christians to give thanks for every circumstance; rather, he was saying that in each circumstance there is a glimmer of hope for which we can be thankful. God is with us. The apostle Paul is big on steering clear of pity parties and focusing instead on the hope of what God can do through our circumstances.

In the Old Testament, the Israelites learned a powerful lesson when they chose to grumble and complain and look at what was wrong in the wilderness. They failed to focus on the great work that God was doing in their lives. He was providing for them day by day—he gave them water and food, and he even made sure that their shoes didn't wear out in the journey. Yet instead of joy, they chose anger. Now, I know their circumstances weren't the best, but they could have made the best of them. Easy for me to say; I wasn't there. But as a casual observer, I can look at the Israelites' situation and learn a lesson about the choice they made concerning their attitude. You and I have the same choice today. I'm guessing your life isn't perfect; nonetheless, there are still things we can smile about.

I'm not saying to deny the fact that you have sadness or problems in your life. It is important to grieve and cry, but it is also important to smile and laugh, and we don't want to overlook the choice to do so. Let's make a decision never to go through a day without smiling in gratitude for some gift God has given us. God's handiwork is all around us—don't miss it! Let's have a perspective of joy and thankfulness. I know we are not placed on this earth simply to have fun. God has a purpose and a plan for each one of us, and we should be about his business first and foremost in our lives. But even Paul, who was serious about his work of spreading the gospel, encouraged us to experience joy and hope in the midst of our life and work.

Uncovering Fun

A fun attitude begins with joy in our hearts and surfaces with an openness to new ideas and creativity. As we unlock our attitudes, we are more apt to see the fun lurking all around us. For instance, a difficult day of moving into a new house can be turned into a castle of fun as you take a large packing box, cut a door, and create a playhouse or tunnel. Sorting laundry can evolve into a game of Match the Socks or Throw the Coupled Socks into the Basket. Waiting at the doctor's office can become a special time to read a new book together or create a new drawing on the sketch pad saved exclusively for waiting-room visits.

We can see our responsibilities with the kids in the dim light of drudgery or in the bright light of ideas. How do we do it? Where do we get fun ideas? I believe it begins with prayer, asking the God of all creation to grant us creative ideas as we spend time with our kids. I know in my own life there were times I was at my wit's end with my two toddler girls, and I would ask the Lord (in desperation) for a fresh or creative idea. In my own experience, a thought would flood my mind, or I would find a new, quick, and doable activity in a book or magazine. Yes, God wants us to seek him even in the small things.

Fun ideas can be found in many different places. Parenting and family magazines are often a wonderful resource for easy ideas. Some local newspapers provide seasonal activities or creative recipes to do with the kids. I've caught new ideas on television shows geared for families. There are times when I'll hear one of my friends talk about something fun she did with her family.

Now, if you're like me, you may see a good idea or hear about a fun family activity but can't put your finger on it when you want it. So I suggest you start a family fun file.

A simple accordion file or a colorful box with file folders is all you need. For me, bright colors are always motivating and inspirational. You may want to label your folders as follows:

Birthday Party Ideas
Fun Kid Recipes
Summer Sensations
Fall Fun
Winter Wonders
Spring Spectacular Ideas
Boredom Busters
Travel Tips

Use the file to organize ideas, recipes, and crafts that you collect from magazines, television shows, or newspapers. When a friend gives me a new idea, I jot it down and put it in the file so I can reference it when I need it. As your kids get older, you may want to weed out some of the old clippings and put in new ones that are more appropriate for their age. Whether it's notes from a parenting seminar or something you heard on the radio, now you will have a fun file as your own personal resource. You'll be surprised at how alert you are to new ideas once you have created a file and determined in your heart that you are going to bless your family with amusement and laughter.

A Fun Mess

Most important, a fun parent is open to hospitality. Yes, an open-door policy invites fun because people know they will be welcomed with a smile into your home. An attitude of "Oh no. What are they going to mess up?" can slightly stifle the expectation of fun times. A home with an inviting atmosphere frees guests up to be themselves and enjoy time together. Life is meant to be enjoyed with others. A game or project comes alive when friends are around but can be a lead balloon by our lonesome.

We can't go through life worrying about the mess! Now, I know that we need to maintain responsibility and not allow people to go wild in our homes, but there is a healthy balance. I have found it helpful to have things on hand to prevent any major messes (such as plastic tablecloths and plenty of coasters for drinks). I have learned that most things clean up fairly easily, and of course people are more important than things. I let my kids know what is expected of them. I also let them know their limits. When my kids were young, I kept some things out of their reach and off-limits. Now that they are older, they know they are responsible for caring for their guests and making sure they are respectful of the furniture and clean up after themselves.

My friend Jennifer wrote a poem when her kids were little concerning mess. Just a little insight into Jennifer—she has a business in which she organizes people's clutter. You can imagine her personality; she is one who enjoys life when all her ducks are in a row. Then she had kids and realized that it's not so easy to maintain a perfect house. Listen to her words:

Blessed Messes
by Jennifer McMahan

You'll find them in the kitchen
And scattered down the hall,

Some are in the closets
And many a bedroom wall,

Some are made of crayon
And others red sticky jelly . . .

But the one I love the most
Is the carpet vermicelli.

Once there was a time when
I would not have been so calm,

But God has changed my heart
And blessed me as a Mom.[1]

Jennifer's poem is a reminder to us all that life is messy, people are messy, and fun is messy, but there are tremendous blessings because of the mess. If we can maintain the outlook of openness to joy, laughter, and fun while ignoring the urge to keep everything perfect, we, too, can experience the wonder of showing hospitality and delighting in the people God has brought into our home.

Portrait of a Fun Mom

What does a fun mom look like? Helen paints a beautiful picture of a fun mom for us. I met Helen last year when I was speaking to a mom's group in Coppell, Texas. She introduced my talk titled "Having a Fun House" with the following message about the moms in her neighborhood when she was growing up, as well as in her current neighborhood. As you read her story, you can't help but ask yourself, "Which kind of mom am I?"

I remember three stay-at-home moms from my childhood street. One mom was basically invisible, doing her own thing. She wasn't mean, but she wasn't welcoming either. Another mom was not terribly friendly. You felt like you were imposing. She was always hovering. She would actually cut pieces of Trident gum in half and give each child one-half of a piece of gum. I always felt that she didn't like me because my parents didn't go to church.

Then there was Mrs. Anderson. I wished that my mom was like her. She was home when her kids were home. She was nice to me. Sometimes she took me to church with her and her family. Mrs. Anderson gave us Kool-Aid, and she let us play in the sprinkler until her yard was one big mud puddle. All the kids on the block were always at her house.

Here in Coppell, I live next door to a Mrs. Anderson. Her house is the "fun house" on my street. There is a constant stream of boys and bicycles up and down the sidewalk. To come out of my driveway, I have to weave my van through the scooters and the air-soft-pellet-gun battles.

I was thinking about Karol's talk on having a fun house, and of course, I thought of my neighbor. So I called my neighbor and asked her why she has a fun house. At first she said, "Well, we have a pool and a trampoline." I pointed out to her that the kids only swim in the summertime. And four out of the six houses on our circle have trampolines, but hers is the one that's in constant use. Then she thought it might have something to do with her child's personality. And I agree with that somewhat. But I felt there was more to it than that. After probing her further, I got some ideas from her. Here are some things to think about if you want your house to be the fun house on your street:

Be encouraging. Make a point to let your child know their friends are welcome. This seems obvious, but sometimes our kids need to have things spelled out for them. Of course, let them know that they should check with you first to see if that particular day works for you. But I think kids pick up on whether you are welcoming to their friends, and then they will be welcoming in turn.

Be available. She's home when her kids are home. This makes other parents OK with letting their kids come over to her house. Some kids don't have someone at home in the afternoons and have rules that they can't have friends over. Or their dad works from home and needs quiet to get work done. Either way, that's not the ideal environment for kids to have fun.

Be prepared. At least in the summer, she has snacks available. You don't have to get elaborate; a bowl of microwave popcorn or a box of Popsicles is fine. During street roller-hockey games, she brings out the water cooler and plastic cups. She has a certain flag with a watermelon slice on it that she hangs by her front door in the summer that means "open swim," which means any neighbor child who sees that flag knows they are welcome to come swim during those times. My kids look for the swim flag as we drive by.

Be relaxed. To an extent, she says she's not that particular about how neat her house is. Of course, she makes the kids clean up after snacks, like throwing away their paper plates. But she turned her formal living room into a game room where the kids can hang out. That's what you see when she opens her front door. And that's OK with her. Think about that for a minute.

Be clear about expectations. Relaxed doesn't mean there are no rules. The kids know not to get on the hardwood floor in a wet bathing suit. Sometimes she's had to post a sign on the door that says her son can't play until 4:30, or whatever time works. But . . .

Be flexible. Your kids change, and so do the seasons. In the winter when it gets dark by 5:30, she lets her kids play first and then do homework after dinner.

Last summer, I went back to my hometown for my high school reunion and I saw Mrs. Anderson's son. He told me his sister was in town visiting and I should call his house the next day to say hi. So I did. I dialed the number from memory, and Mrs. Anderson answered the phone. After having not seen her for more than fifteen years, she immediately asked me if I could come over that morning to see them. I drove over to her house and spent the next hour watching my kids run around the backyard with her grandkids. She is still the fun house.

Proverbs 16:17 says, "The highway of the upright avoids evil; he who guards his way guards his life."

Someday when my kids look back on me as a mom, I want them to think of me the way I think of Mrs. Anderson. I'm going to ask God to guard me and to keep me on the right highway as a mom to achieve that goal.[2]

I couldn't have said it better!

Family Fun Devotional

Read: Isaiah 43:1–5

Talk:

- What do you learn about the Lord's care and love for his people in this passage?
- Knowing that your wonderful Creator loves you so deeply, how does that affect the love you have for other people?
- What does this passage have to say about fear?

Do:

Foil Fun for the Whole Family

Take a roll of aluminum foil and give each family member an eighteen-inch sheet of foil. Tell everyone to scrunch it and form it into an object of some sort. They can use more foil if they like. Set the timer for two minutes. At the end of two minutes, everyone stops. Now it is time to guess what each person created. Most of the time each family member must simply tell what it is, but it sure is fun to try to guess. Talk about the fact that creativity spurs laughter and encourages fun. Thank the Lord for being our loving Creator, and ask him to give us creativity as we reach out to others.

4

Creative Ideas for Every Season

Autumn to winter, winter into spring,
Spring into summer, summer into fall,
So rolls the changing year, and so we change . . .

DINAH MULOCK CRAIK

He has made everything beautiful in its time.

ECCLESIASTES 3:11

When I was a classroom teacher, seasons were everything! We celebrated autumn with browns and oranges and golds. We decorated with leaves, and our handouts had little turkeys, pilgrims, and pumpkins on them. Every season was a new opportunity to change colors, themes, and pictures! The changing of the seasons kept us from getting in a rut and getting bored with the same old stuff. Just when we grew tired of leaves and pilgrims, it was time to switch to snowflakes and wise men.

Hooray for seasons! In this chapter, we are going to explore ways you can create memories in your home one season at a time. I'm all about keeping it simple and enjoyable. (I never really liked those teachers who went overboard with elaborate decorations and over-the-top projects.) Memories are made not from perfect decorations and sophisticated activities but from warm and sensible ideas that increase your joy of the season.

The goal here is not to stress ourselves out over the various holidays and seasons. The goal is to offer a few easy and fresh approaches to celebrate the seasons with our kids and build fond memories in the process. My hope is that some of these ideas stick with you and that you will repeat them year after year. I don't want to overwhelm you with an exhausting amount of ideas and options. In my home, I have several special seasonal decorations, activities, and recipes that I consistently use each year, and I have found that the repetition creates fond traditions for my kids. In fact, if I forget to put out a decoration or carry out a tradition, the kids will eventually ask about it. I feel that these few special things will be the things they look forward to when they come home when they are grown (and bring the grandkids).

You will find I have provided several decorating tips, family activities, and kid-friendly recipes for each season. Pick and choose ones that would make good traditions for your own family. Additionally, I suggest a scent for each season. Why? Because fond memories are built through the use of all of our senses. In our home, I decorate each season with a certain scent (using candles, oil, or potpourri) that my family can remember and expect each year. Even if you don't use my exact suggestions, it is my hope that I will spur on your own creativity, which you can apply to your family's interests and personality.

Summer Sensations

Summer can end up being the best of times, but it can also be the worst of times if kids are hot and bored. You can make it the best of times for your family by taking the opportunity to enjoy the great outdoors.

Summer Activities

Sidewalk Chalk. Never underestimate the fun of sidewalk chalk for kids of any age. This inexpensive activity offers myriad ideas for creativity. Hopscotch, foursquare, artistic masterpieces, and human-sized tic-tac-toe are just a few of the things you can do with just a little chalk on a nice summer evening.

Sprinkler Mania. One of my fondest memories growing up was playing in the sprinklers in our front yard. All the kids from the neighborhood would gather at the sprinklers for relief from the heat. For just a few dollars at Wal-Mart, you can create summer water fun for your kids and the entire neighborhood. Purchase either the whirling sprinkler or the one that spreads (like a rake) and moves back and forth. Turn the water on at a low pressure and allow everyone to jump over the sprinkler. Raise the height, and add to the challenge. Or play tag right through the sprinkler.

Fourth of July Parade. Organize or participate in the neighborhood Independence Day parade. Decorate bikes, trikes, and strollers with crepe paper, flags, pinwheels, etc. Place flags along the parade route. In our neighborhood, we chose one house for the beginning and end of the parade. We played patriotic music on a portable CD player; provided lemonade, water, and doughnuts; and chose one special car to be the head of the parade. It was simple and special, and it provided a wonderful gathering for neighbors.

Summer Recipes
Breakfast Pizza

2 cans crescent rolls

1–2 lbs. sausage

6–8 eggs

Shredded cheese (your family's favorite variety)

Preheat oven to temperature on the crescent rolls can. Smooth out crescent rolls over an entire cookie sheet, making sure all seams are smoothed together. Brown sausage, then crumble into small pieces and sprinkle over crust. Scramble eggs and distribute over crust. Sprinkle cheese over pizza. Bake for 16 to 18 minutes or until browned. Serve with salsa or ketchup.

Sensational Summer Salad

1 7-oz. pkg. bowtie pasta	⅓ cup green onions, sliced
1 6½-oz. can tuna	¼ cup chopped fresh parsley
1 medium tomato, chopped	¾ cup Italian dressing
1 green or yellow pepper,	1–2 tsp. Dijon mustard
cut into strips	½ tsp. salt
½ cup whole pitted black olives	¼ tsp. lemon pepper
8–10 radishes, sliced	

Cook pasta according to directions on package. Drain. Combine pasta, tuna, tomato, pepper, olives, radishes, green onions, and parsley. In a small bowl, mix remaining ingredients. Add to pasta/tuna mixture. Toss gently. Cover and chill.

Happy-Face Ice Cream Sundaes

Favorite flavors of ice cream
Variety of candies and marshmallows
Chocolate or caramel syrup

Place a large scoop of ice cream in a bowl. Squirt or drizzle syrup at the top of the scoop to resemble hair. Place candy or marshmallows to create eyes, nose, and mouth. Allow each family member to create his or her own. Vote on the most creative work of art before eating them.

Summer Decorating Tips

Since Memorial Day comes at the beginning of summer vacation, followed by Flag Day and the Fourth of July, consider creating an American theme for your decorations. Over the years, I have begun to collect ceramic red, white, and blue pitchers, mugs, and even salt and pepper shakers. I place flags throughout the house (in planters) and around the yard. I even bought a large wooden Uncle Sam figure that holds a sign saying "A Patriotic Welcome," which I place at our front door each year. Other summer decorating may include a strawberry theme or bold, bright flowers.

Summer Scent

Orange/vanilla or lemon verbena

Fall Fun

Back to school, football games, changing colors, crisp cool air, and Thanksgiving all seem to blend together when I think of autumn. As we slowly change directions from the carefree spirit of summer, we begin to enjoy the warmth of a new season. The activities and responsibilities that come with the beginning of school can keep us running with a new routine and a bit of a busier schedule. Here are some ways to build wonderful family time and fall memories.

Fall Activities

Waxed Paper Leaves. On a family walk or nature scavenger hunt, collect beautifully colored fallen leaves and acorns. You may want to take several walks during the week to build a wonderful collection. Use some of the leaves and acorns to decorate your kitchen table. Place your favorite leaves in between large squares of waxed paper. Place the waxed paper between two hand towels and iron (medium to hot temperature) so the wax melts together and encloses the leaves. Cut out construction-paper frames to surround the pictures. Decorate a kitchen window with your new creations.

Roasted Pumpkin Seeds. Pumpkins are certainly plentiful around the end of October. I usually purchase a few for fall decorations around our house; then at some point we gut out the goop. This is a fun, messy activity to do together outside with the pumpkins on newspapers. Once you have carefully cut open the pumpkin (and put the knife safely away), allow your kids to help you scoop out the seeds with their hands and place the seeds and gunk in a colander. Rinse and dry the pumpkin seeds. Sauté in butter. Add seasonings to taste. Place the seeds on a cookie sheet with sides, and roast on low broil for several minutes on each side.

Orange Turkeys. You will need an orange for each child, plus toothpicks, gumdrops, and construction paper. Create the beautiful fan of a turkey's tail by skewering a variety of colors of gumdrops on five or six toothpicks. Stick the toothpicks in a row on the orange, and this becomes the turkey's tail. You can make a head with a beard using construction paper. Glue the head to a toothpick and insert it at the end opposite the tail. Finally, use three toothpicks in the bottom of the orange to make the turkey stand on its own. Decorate your Thanksgiving table with your creations.

Fall Recipes

Cinnamon Pumpkin Cake

4 eggs	1 tsp. cinnamon
1 cup oil	1 tsp. nutmeg
3 cups sugar	½ tsp. baking powder
1 cup water	2 tsp. soda
3½ cups flour	16 oz. can pumpkin pie filling
1 tsp. cloves	

Mix eggs, oil, sugar, and water. Mix dry ingredients and

gradually add to the egg mixture. After mixing well, add pumpkin and continue mixing. Spray a Bundt pan or tube pan with nonstick spray. Bake in a preheated 350-degree oven for 1 hour and 15 minutes. Allow to cool completely and then remove from pan.

Corn Spoon Bread

1 stick butter or margarine
1 pkg. Jiffy cornbread mix
1 egg
8 oz. sour cream
1 16-oz. can whole kernel corn, drained

Melt butter. Combine all ingredients in a bowl and mix well. Pour into an 8x8 inch baking dish. Bake at 350 degrees for 30 to 40 minutes until set and lightly browned on top.

Pecan-Crusted Chicken

4 chicken breast halves, skinless and boneless
½ cup honey Dijon salad dressing
1 cup finely chopped pecans

Flatten each piece of chicken by placing it between waxed paper and beating it or rolling it to about ¼ inch thickness. Spread dressing on both sides of chicken, and dredge chicken in chopped pecans. Place chicken in a lightly greased shallow baking dish. Bake at 350 degrees for 30 minutes or until tender. Makes 4 servings.

Fall Decorating Tips

Fall leaves, acorns, nuts, and apples make a wonderful, natural way to decorate. I use a garland of silk leaves and plastic or wooden apples, which can be used year after year. Over the years I've also collected a few Pilgrim figurines, cornucopias, and a beautiful pumpkin pitcher that I bring out each fall. You can also decorate with beautiful baskets of mums, pumpkins, and picture books that tell of our nation's forefathers.

Fall Scent

Sugar cookie, apple pie, or pumpkin spice

Winter Wonders

Winter is experienced differently in different places around the world. Some may experience heavy snow and extreme cold, while others get excited when they have the opportunity to see a few flurries. No matter where we live, we still tend to think of winter in terms of Christmas, snowmen, and gingerbread houses, so we will use them all as part of our winter celebration.

Winter Activities

Caroling. Whether it's in your neighborhood or at a local nursing home, you can give the gift of Christmas joy to others by organizing a group of carolers. Consider inviting neighborhood or church kids over for a caroling party. Serve hot chocolate and cookies while you practice a few carols together, and then venture out and bless others with your singing. In our neighborhood, we gathered kids together with one mom who could play the guitar. We journeyed to each house on our street. The joy that we brought our neighbors gave us each a blessing as well. Not to mention the fact that we all grew closer to one another as we sang together.

Gingerbread House. Graham crackers, cake icing, candy canes, and gumdrops are all you need to create an afternoon full of fun and a memorable activity. We buy the kits that have all of the essentials in one box. Making a gingerbread house offers you a blessed family time together and the opportunity to use your creative energy. You may even consider having a contest with another family or within yours. Be sure to take a picture so you can look back over the years of houses and memories.

Theme Trees. Each year we decorate a small tree in our kitchen with a new and unique theme. As a family, we begin thinking about the theme in early November and collecting items here and there for the tree. One year during the Beanie Babies craze, we had a Beanie Babies tree filled with the beanie toys of all sizes and colored lights. One year we did an American tree, another year a cowboy tree. We've also had a New York tree (after a Thanksgiving trip to New York), a candy cane tree, and an angel tree. We have fun preparing and decorating the theme tree, and our guests always enjoy seeing what we do each year.

Christmas Eve Chili and Tamales. Every Christmas Eve, we open our doors to family and friends after the Christmas Eve church service. We serve tamales and chili and enjoy warm fellowship. It's easy to do, and we never know who will come. I'm not sure why this has become a tradition except that it is nice to have a Southwest meal before the traditional turkey dinner. We always serve chili con carne (chili with meat). Once I heard a pastor say that chili con carne on Christmas Eve reminds us of God Con Carne (God with flesh), Jesus.

Winter Recipes

Green Eggs and Ham

6 eggs
¾ cup milk
Green food coloring
Ham slices

Beat eggs and milk until well blended. Add several drops of green food coloring. Pour into pan over medium heat. Scramble eggs until preferred texture. Serve with ham slices. This red and green breakfast has become a Christmas morning tradition at our home every year.

Cranberry Coffeecake

½ cup margarine

1 cup walnut or pecan pieces

2½ cups white sugar

1 cup brown sugar

1 can whole cranberries

1 box yellow cake mix

eggs and oil (according to cake mix instructions)

Slice margarine into thin slices and arrange evenly in the bottom of a 9x13 inch pan. Sprinkle nuts over the butter. In a separate bowl, combine white and brown sugar. Add cranberries and toss lightly. Distribute sugared cranberries evenly over nut layer. Prepare yellow cake mix batter according to directions and pour batter over cranberries. Bake at 350 degrees for 40 minutes or until toothpick inserted in the center comes out clean. Cool 10 minutes; loosen edges with a knife and turn pan over on a platter. Slice into small squares and serve with whipped cream.

Cola-Baked Brisket

1 4–6 lb. boneless beef brisket

1 onion, sliced

1 can cola

Salt and pepper

1 garlic clove, chopped

Place sliced onions in the bottom of a roasting pan. Sprinkle both sides of brisket with salt and pepper and place, fat side up, on top of the onions. Prick brisket several times with a fork. Slowly pour cola over brisket. Season with garlic and cover with aluminum foil. Bake at 325 degrees for 4 to 4½ hours, basting occasionally. Serve on a large platter; garnish with onions.

Winter Decorations

Winter can be beautifully adorned with pinecones and holly branches. It's fun to spray-paint pinecones or add glitter and use them as decorations. You can decorate with snow by taking a simple glass globe or bowl and pouring Epsom salts in the bottom. You can place a figurine or a small blue votive candle in the center. Decorating with special Nativity scenes and Christmas books can also add to the holiday spirit. Each year I add either a beautiful Christmas book or an angel or Nativity scene. I have some lovely Christmas picture books that not only make beautiful decorations but also are fun to look at (like the one with pictures of Christmas celebrated around the world).

Lights and music also add to the holiday spirit. You may want to purchase several classical or serene Christmas music CDs when they are half price after the holidays so that you can have them for the next year. Lights are beautiful outside, but you may want to have a few inside on a tree or doorway just to add a special effect to the inside of your home. Again, buy them after the season and save them for the next year (if you can remember where you put them!).

Winter Scent

Cinnamon or cranberry

Spring Spectacular

Spring is a time of new beginnings. The freshness of the season and the celebration of our risen Lord offer wonderful reasons to enjoy this season.

Spring Activities

Decorated Flowerpots. Purchase several inexpensive clay pots. Place the pots on newspaper and spray-paint them or hand-paint them. Once they dry, you can add rickrack, stickers, trim, and/or glitter. You can write a Bible verse or a poem on them with Sharpie pens.

Pleasant Planting. Visit the local nursery and allow each child to have a designated amount they can spend on a plant. Give them twenty minutes to find the one they want. Younger ones will need your assistance, while older ones can read up or inquire about the care involved with the plant. Take the purchases home, and work together to plant them either in the ground or in their newly decorated pots. Teach the kids responsibility in taking care of the plant and watering it regularly.

Kite Adventures. Go for a kite-flying adventure, and be sure to take the camera. It's more fun with the whole family! After you enjoy flying kites, return home to create a colorful construction-paper kite. You may even want to put a picture of your kite-flying adventure on your newly constructed craft kite. Top off the day by watching *Mary Poppins.*

Clouds. Take a bedroll and pillows outside, and lie down and look up. Watch the clouds, and point out figures and pictures that you see in them. After a while you may want to come inside and make a cloud picture using blue construction paper and white chalk or cotton balls and glue.

Spring Recipes

Easter Morning Rolls

2 cups self-rising flour
2 cups vanilla ice cream, softened

Lightly stir ingredients together until just moistened. Line muffin tins with paper liners. Fill three-fourths full.

Bake at 325 degrees for 20 minutes. Yields 16 to 20 muffins. We use these muffins as an Easter tradition at our home and talk about how the rolls symbolically represent Christ, the Bread of Life. The muffins have two ingredients, just as Christ is made up of both God and man. The white color represents his purity, and the flour is self-rising (which represents our Easter celebration of Christ's rising from the dead).

Flower-Face Sandwiches

Bread
Favorite sandwich ingredients
Flower-shaped cookie cutters
Celery or zucchini strips
Spanish olives (stuffed with pimento)
Small tomatoes and or carrots

Make several of your favorite sandwiches, and then cut them into floral shapes using your cookie cutter. Add veggie strips to be the stalks of the flowers. Create a face on each sandwich using sliced olives, tomatoes, and/or carrots.

Ice Cream Flowerpots

4–6 small clay flowerpots (thoroughly washed)
½ gallon vanilla or chocolate ice cream
2 cups chocolate cookie crumbs
Gummy worms (optional)
4–6 plastic flowers

Soften ice cream. Line the bottoms of the pots with waxed paper or foil. Pour softened ice cream into pots (adding gummy worms if desired). Cover ice cream with cookie crumbs. Stick one plastic flower in the top of each pot. Place ice cream flowerpots in the freezer for several hours.

Spring Decorations

Springtime shouts with bright flowers and bold colors. Create a fun Gerber daisy centerpiece for your kitchen table, or add daisies throughout your home in baskets with greenery. For springtime, I love to use brightly colored tablecloths, place mats, and napkins. You can add spring delight by adding simple things such as bright picture frames, ribbon, and green or blue glass vases with fresh flowers.

Spring Scent

Freesia or fresh floral scents

Seasonal Summary

As you pull together thoughts and ideas to bless your home, keep in mind that the point is not to do everything to perfection. It is more important to celebrate the time together and create fond memories. Our plans of perfection are worthless if we do not decorate our lives with a loving attitude and flexible spirit. A recipe may flop or a decoration may crumble, but a heart that is filled with love covers it all up. So embrace each season, but more important, embrace one another and allow Christ's love to pour through you to family and friends.

Family Fun Devotional

Read: Daniel 2:20–23

Talk:
- Who is in charge of the times and the seasons?
- Which season are you most thankful for?
- Take time to praise and thank God as a family for the beauty of the seasons and the wonder of his ways and timing.

Do:
Choose one of the seasonal activities listed in this chapter that fits with the current season, and do it as a family. Take pictures and make a scrapbook page of the memory together.

Boredom Busters

The man who lets himself be bored is even more contemptible than the bore.

SAMUEL BUTLER

He who pursues righteousness and love finds life, prosperity and honor.

PROVERBS 21:21

For many years we had a tradition in our home. On the first day of summer vacation, we gathered around the kitchen table, ate doughnuts, and planned our summer. We started with a big poster board bearing the words "Super Summer 2001" (or whatever year it was at the time). Then using different colored markers, we would write down some of the activities we wanted to do during the summer, such as go to Six Flags, play putt-putt golf, and ice-skate. We also wrote down some of the obligations of the summer, such as "Read for forty-five minutes each day" or "Only one hour of television per day." I, of course, established the obligations, but I introduced them in a semipleasant way as we created the poster together.

Then we would pull out the boredom buster can. This was an old coffee can that I decorated years ago. It had a slit in the tip of the lid in which we could place boredom-busting ideas. We cleaned out the can from year to year so we could add new, fresh ideas. My daughters and I sat around the kitchen table with little pieces of paper and talked about the different things we could do if we ever felt the "B" word (*boredom*) coming into our minds.

As we thought about ideas, we would write them down and put them in the can so that at any time we could pick one, read it, and remind ourselves of things we could do. We wrote down things such as bake cookies, shoot hoops, jump on the trampoline, call a friend, go swimming, write a letter to a relative, and so on. It was a great exercise because it made us realize that with a little thought and creativity, there was plenty to do—always.

Oddly, we never had to open the can during the summer, because we had already thought through what was in there. We went ahead and did the activities we remembered writing down, and we were never at a loss for something to do. The fact is, boredom is in the eye of the beholder. If you let yourself mope around and declare yourself bored, then there you are. But boredom is simply a perspective. There is always something positive to do with your time, even if it is doing nothing.

Relaxing Is Good; Laziness Is Not

How do you handle those times when you have nothing to do? We live in a society that glorifies busyness. The more you do, the more esteemed you are, so we overbook our kids' lives (especially their summers), fearing they will become lazy and bored. The end result is that we run ourselves and our kids into a frazzled, tired mess, all for the fear of dreaded boredom. The fact many of us fail to realize is that overscheduling is not healthy either.

The misconception comes in equating "nothing to do" with

boredom to the point that we have lost our ability to relax. All of us need downtime. We need time for creativity and rejuvenation. We need empty space in our schedule, not to grow bored but to learn to be productive. We certainly don't want to raise lazy kids, but we need to recognize the difference between unscheduled time and laziness.

Webster's defines the verb *bore* as "to weary by being dull, uninteresting, or monotonous," and *boredom* is "the condition of being bored or uninterested." By definition, boredom is not the lack of stuff to do but rather being too dull and uninteresting to use your time wisely or creatively. The burden of boredom rests with the boredee (my personal term for the person who claims he is bored).

In our home, I taught my daughters that they were not allowed to say the "B" word, not because it was naughty but because it is an embarrassing indictment of the person who says it. When a person says, "I'm bored," what they are really saying is, "I'm too dull and uninteresting to think of anything to do." Being bored is a very unbecoming quality.

We need to help our kids see that being alone or having nothing to do can be a good thing. There is a way to teach our kids how to relax and rejuvenate without being lazy. Even God stressed to the Israelites that they should work six days a week and rest one day a week. God established a pattern for deliberate resting; why not teach our kids to do the same?

Proverbs teaches quite a bit about laziness and also about being a diligent worker. Let's teach our kids the value of hard work and relaxing, while helping them understand the problems that result from being lazy. Giving our kids age-appropriate chores instills a strong work ethic, builds ingenuity, and prevents boredom. During the summer especially, as they have a little more time on their hands, give them a few practical chores to do, but also give them time to relax. You may want to ask them what relaxes them. It may be reading a book or playing music or watching a movie. Allow them to have that downtime after they have accomplished their daily chores.

Practical Solutions to Boredom

Ultimately, boredom is blaming others for what we should be taking care of ourselves. We want our kids to understand that they don't have to depend on someone else for their entertainment and fun. Personal entertainment and enjoyment can come in many forms and fashions, such as playing games, doing crafts or activities, spending time with friends, hiking, biking, reading, drawing, or listening to music.

Let's open up our kids' minds to what they can do! As parents, we must be wise to have some restrictions as to what our kids may or may not do. I think sometimes we fear for our kids to have downtime because we are afraid they may get into trouble. Let me assure you that we can set parameters while still allowing lots of room for creativity. For instance, we may not object to our kids' watching television, but sitting there for endless hours watching who knows what is not healthy or good. So you set a boundary of watching only a limited amount of television, letting the kids know the shows that are off-limits. If you find that they have crossed the boundary lines, a natural consequence and punishment could be that they lose the television privilege for a certain period of time.

It's our job to give our children opportunities to use their imagination and creativity. Here are a few quick and easy boredom-busting activities that can stretch and develop our kids' creative thinking skills.

Boredom-Busting Arts and Crafts

Morning Sketches. A large, blank sketch or art pad can allow our kids to open up their minds to draw new ideas or express thoughts and emotions. Just after breakfast, while the mind is fresh with new thoughts and ideas, is a good time to hand out sketch pads. A variety of markers, crayons, colored pencils, and watercolors adds variety to art. You may choose to use a different medium each day or each week. I'm always on the lookout for nice sketch pads or art paper on sale in the clearance section of hobby or craft stores. You can also purchase special watercolor art pads and paper.

Trash Art. Don't throw away cereal boxes, plastic jugs, and aluminum cans! They are works of art in the making. You can use them as building blocks to create a castle. You can spray-paint them and decorate them with sequins and jewels. You can cut away the top of the jug to make a planter or a knick-knack bowl. Take a giant box outside and let the kids paint it. They can paint the whole thing one color, or they can paint pictures all over it and create a collection of masterpieces.

Duct Tape Creations. One time for a long car trip we gave each of the girls (and their two friends) a roll of duct tape and scissors and told them to create something. We encouraged them to think outside the box and design some sort of usable object with the duct tape. One girl made a wallet (which she still uses to this day), one made a pair of flip-flops, and two of the girls made the most unique purses you have ever seen. Loads of simple, inexpensive fun from a roll of tape!

Boredom-Busting Activities

The Wonder of a Sheet. Never underestimate the activities that you can do using a large bedsheet. Drape a sheet over a card table or kitchen table or large umbrella, and you can create an instant fort or playhouse. All the kids need to do is add some of their toys and their imaginations. You can also use a bedsheet for an indoor picnic or for a parachute game outside. The parachute game works best with at least five to six kids. Everyone stands in a circle and holds the edges of the sheet. You can circle in one direction, then in another. You can bounce an inflated ball or a stuffed animal. My favorite is to make the sheet mushroom up (by holding it high above our heads and then bringing the edges slowly down), and then everyone sits under the sheet as they bring it down around them.

Extraordinary Interviews. Using a tape recorder or videocamera, have the kids pretend they are on-the-street reporters or interviewing a celebrity. Make a microphone by using an empty toilet-paper tube with a small ball of crumpled foil at the top. Cover the whole thing with foil, and you have an instant interview. You can ask silly questions to each other and take turns being the interviewer and interviewee. It's always fun to watch or listen to the interviews too.

Boredom Busters in the Kitchen

Magnificent Mac. Take the tried-and-true macaroni and cheese recipe to a new level. The fun is not only in the making but in adding a variety of ingredients to personalize this macaroni and cheese recipe.

> 2 cups dried macaroni or pasta (choose your favorite shapes)
> 12 oz. American cheese (3 cups shredded)
> 2 Tbsp. butter or margarine
> 2 Tbsp. all-purpose flour
> ⅛ tsp. black pepper
> 2½ cups milk

Cook pasta according to directions on package. Drain and set aside. While pasta is cooking, grate the cheese (allow older kids to help). Melt butter in a medium-sized pan. Gradually stir in flour and pepper. Add milk. Stir and cook over medium heat until slightly thickened and a little bubbly. Slowly add cheese and stir until melted. Add pasta to the cheese mixture. Place in a 2-quart casserole dish. Bake at 350 degrees uncovered for 25 to 30 minutes.

Now that you have your wonderful cheesy noodles, consider adding your favorite extras to the top. Consider cubes of ham, little wieners, potato chips, carrots, another type of cheese, fried onion rings, shoestring potatoes, or goldfish crackers.

No Reason Cake. Most of the time we have a reason to bake a cake, whether it is someone's birthday or a shower or special occasion. It's a good idea to have a box of cake mix and a couple of cans of icing in your pantry at all times as a potential boredom buster. Making the cake is always fun, especially if you offer to let the kids stir and lick the bowl and spoons. Then comes the joy of icing the cake! Once the cake is iced by all of your little helpers, allow everyone to come up with ways to decorate the top. You may want to choose a random theme. The possibilities are endless (as long as you clean them well): toy soldiers, rubber duckies, small plastic dolls, candies of all sorts, little paper umbrellas, plastic flowers, etc. Enjoy making and eating your innovative creation.

Boredom Busters for Waiting Rooms

Picture-Perfect Stories. Look around the room in which you are waiting. Typically, there will be at least one picture on the wall. If there is more than one picture, allow your kids to pick one picture for this activity. Tell your kids to give careful observation to the picture and the objects or people in the picture. (You may want to give them a certain time period.) Now they must create a story about what they see. They can either write it down or tell it to you. Depending on how long your wait may be, have them draw a picture (on a paper place mat or pad of paper) showing what happens next in the story.

Special Treasures. If you know you are going to be in a situation where you will be waiting quite a bit, create a special bag for your waiting-room visits. The tote bag should be equipped with objects, small toys, and games that are saved especially for the waiting-room bag, since overfamiliarity with a toy breeds contempt. Suggested treasures for your bag may include a small Etch A Sketch, a fun coloring book or activity book with glitter crayons, a small book or game, a small doll or action figure, a small puzzle, a kid magazine, a play telephone, flash cards, and snacks if appropriate.

Homemade Book. You can make your own picture book and save it for waiting-room visits. Purchase an inexpensive photo album. Cut out pictures from magazines, posters, brochures, even cereal or diaper boxes. Put them in the album, covered with plastic so that little hands can touch the pictures. Add simple words for the reading-aged kids. You can also make a touch-and-feel book by visiting the remnant table at a fabric store and getting little clips of a variety of different fabrics. Cut them in different shapes or glue them to pictures to make a special book designed by Mom. For older kids, you may want to save a special book or magazine to give them when you go on a trip or to a long doctor's appointment.

Blessed Relaxing

Finally, be deliberate about relaxation. As a camp counselor, I saw the value of an intentional R&R time. We called it FOB (flat on back or flat on bunk). This was a time when campers and counselors took a break from the normal routine of the day and simply enjoyed some downtime. The time could be used to rest, write a letter, read, plan, or think. I found it to be such a valuable time that when I became a mom myself, I instituted FOB during the summers when my daughters were elementary-school age. It was a healthy time of rejuvenation that allowed them to see the value of relaxing. It also allowed time for thought and creativity.

Possibly one of the most valuable boredom busters is an obvious, easy, and simple idea: encourage a love for reading great books. My philosophy for kids as well as adults is that you will never be bored if you have a good book to read. Consider making a trip to a discount or half-price bookstore as a family. Give each child a few dollars, and encourage them to find their own treasures. Once you ignite the joy of reading in a person, they will never use the "B" word again.

Our job as parents is not to fill each waking moment so our kids won't be bored. Rather, our job is to teach our kids how to be creative and resourceful so that they don't depend on or blame other people for their happiness or lack thereof. This important life lesson begins under our roof as we inspire our kids to use the gifts and talents God has given them.

Family Fun Devotional

Read: Proverbs 26:13–16. Also read the definition of *bore* or *boredom* in the dictionary or in this chapter.

Talk:

- What do people really mean when they say they are bored?
- In what ways are lazy people similar to people who say they are bored?
- What activities do you enjoy most when you are at home with nothing scheduled?

Do:

Create a boredom busters can using a coffee can. Spray-paint the can or cover it with construction paper, and allow the kids to decorate it using markers, stickers, glue, and sequins. Explain the purpose of the can. Have everyone in the family contribute several ideas of what they can do if they ever start feeling bored. Explain why the "B" word is no longer allowed in your home. Then if you want, make a trip to a discount or half-price bookstore and give everyone a few dollars, allowing them to go on their own treasure hunt for boredom busters.

6

Stuff to Have on Hand
for Quick and Easy Fun

*Make preparations in advance. You never have trouble if
you are prepared for it.*

THEODORE ROOSEVELT

*A prudent person foresees the danger ahead and takes
precautions; the simpleton goes blindly on and suffers the
consequences.*

PROVERBS 22:3 NLT

Oh, the joy when eight of my daughter's friends walk through
my front door, and I have soft drinks, chips, and cookies to offer
them. Oh, the terror when eight hungry kids walk through my
front door and all I have is stale chips, old orange juice, and
moldy cheese in the fridge. Trust me, I've lived through both scenarios. I'll take the first one anytime.

Honestly, sometimes I read Proverbs 31 and sneer at the
description of the perfect wife. But you have to hand it to her;
she was prepared for everything, and I certainly see the value in
that! When it comes to being the fun mom, we need to have a
good supply of food, fun, and potential laughter on hand in

order to be ready for the opportunities that may present themselves. Often we don't have adequate warning when kids are coming over to our house, but we can be prepared for them no matter when they arrive.

There are two major areas of preparedness for being the "fun mom": we need to be ready with activities and stocked with sustenance. Let me assure you that you don't have to be wealthy to have a storehouse of fun and hospitality. You do have to be rich with a spirit of hospitality and generous with a smile, but as far as the stuff, you can be very economical and frugal. Take it from me, the queen of "never pay full price for anything." I will show you how to be ready without emptying your bank account.

Stocked with Sustenance

The key to being prepared with great food is having things that will keep for a while. Below are a few entertaining foods that you can have on hand. Please understand that you do not need to have every one of these items. These are suggestions that you will need to adjust to fit your family and their friends. Certainly little frozen quiches wouldn't be great for preschool gatherings or the football team on Friday night, but they would be helpful when you have a few teenage girls over for brunch or breakfast. So pick and choose; I'm just revealing some of your options. Of course, they can also be enjoyed by your family if the items are hanging around too long. Just don't forget to replace what you use.

In the freezer:
    Hot dogs
    Hamburger patties
    Buns and bread
    Frozen pizza
    Little quiches

stuff to have on hand for quick and easy fun

Popsicles and frozen treats
Ice cream
Ice
Girl Scout cookies
Frozen cookie dough

On the shelf:
Chips (individual bags stay fresh longer)
Peanut butter
Crackers
Vanilla wafers
Popcorn
Trail mix
Brownie mix
Cake mix and icing in a can
Muffin mix
Variety of two-liter soft drinks
Canned chili and Velveeta cheese for queso dip
Kool-Aid or lemonade mix
Mac and cheese in a box
Fruit cups

In the fridge:
Ketchup and mustard
Pickles
Jelly
Cheese (small or individual packages of cheese last longer)
Slice-and-bake cookie dough
Sour cream and onion dip
Ranch dressing
Veggies
Variety of soft drink cans and water bottles (buy what is on sale
    each week)

Pudding or Jell-O cups
Juice boxes

On the kitchen counter:
Cookie jar (with fresh, homemade, healthy cookies)
Fruit (especially apples and oranges)
Candy dish (I usually buy candy that I don't particularly like so
I won't be tempted to eat it all myself)

In the drawers:
Ziploc bags
Aluminum foil
Scissors
Paper towels
Paper plates and cups

Keeping it economical:
Buy in large quantity.
Be on the lookout for special store sales and triple coupon offers.
Purchase postholiday candy.

Ready with Activities

Pick and choose what works for your family and friends. You
don't need everything listed here, but the list will help you think
about some basic items you may need to have on hand to keep
fun alive and thriving in your house. The following items are not
necessarily expensive, electric, or elaborate, but they do offer
years of fun.

Games

Favorite and fun age-appropriate board games
  Classics such as checkers, chess, bingo, dominoes, and playing
    cards
  Popular games such as Monopoly, Life, Cranium, Catch Phrase
  One or two fad games (usually based on current television shows)
Balls of all shapes and sizes
  Essentials: soccer ball, baseball, beach ball
  Others: football, basketball, volleyball, kick ball
Bat and gloves
Cones to be used for boundaries or goalposts
Badminton set
Sidewalk chalk
Plastic bowling set
Small tabletop versions of pool, shuffleboard, or foosball
Bubble formula and bubble makers
Dress-up barrel full of old clothes (to be used for playing
  dress-up or skits)
Puppets
Rope for tug-of-war or jumping
Personal jump rope or Chinese jump rope
Musical instruments

Crafts

Construction paper, all colors and sizes
Stickers, sequins, and jewels
Glue, tape, and stapler
Markers, crayons, and colored pencils
Age-appropriate scissors
Yarn, string, and ribbon scraps
Fabric scraps
Cotton balls and Q-tips
Glitter (if you dare)

Cardboard saved from boxes
Old magazines and greeting cards
Stack of newspapers (to protect surfaces as well as for projects)
Waxed paper

Movies

Keep a collection of old classics and family favorites.
Purchase previously viewed movies on sale at video stores.
Sell or give away old ones that your family has grown out of.
Start a tradition of watching certain favorites on holidays.
Give your family one new movie each Christmas.

Books

Large, interesting picture books
Guinness Book of World Records
Greatest Moments in Sports
Fun and unique picture books for kids
Conversation starter books
Table Talk by Karol Ladd (Broadman & Holman, 2000)
Sticky Situations by Betsy Schmitt (Tyndale, 1997)
Joke and riddle books
Kids' craft books
Skit books
Mind bender and brain game books
Coloring books
Puzzle books (search and find, mazes, and crossword puzzles)
Songbooks or music books

Secret Stash

Some things are best to keep out of the way so that your family (or you for that matter) won't consume them. For instance, I find it helpful to purchase bags of Halloween candy after October 31, when they are on sale dirt cheap. I buy the candy to have it available when we have guests over, so I need to keep it out of the hands of family for a while. In our house, I keep a basket of these goodies on a high, difficult-to-reach shelf. This is the off-limits, "out of sight, out of mind" basket to be used only for guests. You may or may not choose to let your family know that it is there. You know your family!

Vital Resources

There are certain resources that money can't buy, yet they are essential if you are going to have a fun home. A gracious spirit is invaluable as you allow people to enter your home. Always keep a tender heart toward the needs of your visitors whether the needs are emotional, physical, or spiritual. Ask the Lord to give you discernment and wisdom as to how you can offer hospitality to your guests.

The Christlike love and warmth you show to the guests in your home will draw them back time and time again. Overlook little things such as spilled milk, dirty sinks, or not-so-perfectly nutritious meals, and keep your eye on the bigger picture of loving the people who walk in your door. Service with a smile doesn't always come easily. We may not feel like gracefully receiving guests at inconvenient times. That's why we need the Lord's strength and love.

We are weak, but He is strong. We don't have the resources it takes to be a fun person on our own. The most important resource we can have is God's Holy Spirit at work in our lives. I don't know about you, but many times I'm at a loss to discern people's needs or to reach out with the warmth of a smile. I need God's love and grace pouring through me. I need his strength and discernment to help me. I'm guessing you do too.

If you are willing, pray along with me: *Wonderful Lord, thank you for your love, forgiveness, strength, and power. I confess I try to do so much in my own strength, but I fall short. I need you. Oh strong and loving heavenly Father, please grant me the grace and love to enjoy the people in my home. Give me wisdom to find ways to laugh and enjoy my family and friends. Create joy and laughter in our home, and use me as a vessel to encourage these wonderful times together. Shine your light through me. In Jesus's name, amen.*

Family Fun Devotional

Read: Romans 12:12–13

Talk:

- What are ways we can show God's love to the people who come to our home?
- What resources do we need to be ready for fun in our home?
- Why is it important for us to show hospitality (have an open door) to others?

Do:

As a family, review the fun resources you already have, and then decide on one or a few resources you want or could use from the activities section of this chapter. Make a plan to visit local garage sales, flea markets, or bargain stores in order to look for this fun resource. You may be surprised to find several treasures you could use. This activity not only helps you have an item or two on hand but also encourages creativity, thoughtfulness, and hospitality in your family members. The fun is in the hunt! Make it a contest to find the best bargain possible.

step
two

Enjoy Family Time

A happy family is but an earlier heaven.

JOHN BOWRING

Finally, all of you should be of one mind, full of sympathy toward each other, loving one another with tender hearts and humble minds.

1 PETER 3:8 NLT

Fond, lifelong memories are strengthened through the happy times that families experience together.

Terrific Travel Tips

No family should attempt an auto trip if the kids outnumber the car windows.

TERESA BLOOMINGDALE

Lead me in the right path, O LORD . . .
Tell me clearly what to do,
and show me which way to turn.

PSALM 5:8 NLT

When someone asks me to describe my fondest childhood memories, I always respond with the vacations we took as a family. Some of you share similar fond memories, while some of you have only horror stories as you recollect those times of family togetherness. Yes, family travels can be terrific—or they can be terrifying. Although often the unforeseen can arise on a vacation, we still have the ability to take any vacation and make it a great vacation.

What makes a terrific vacation? There are three main ingredients for success. It begins with *wise planning*. I know that the best-laid plans can (or will) go awry, so the next ingredient for terrific vacations is to *flexiblility*. The third ingredient for success is *a good attitude*. Honestly, it doesn't really matter where you go, what you do, or what happens along the way; if you have these three ingredients, you will most likely have a successful trip.

"What?" you may be saying. "We don't need lots of money, first-class tickets, and a luxury hotel to have a successful family vacation?" No! In fact, I know many people who can attest to the fact that extravagance won't guarantee a good vacation. The material stuff is not essential. Even the destination is not all that important. It's the preparation, the flexibility, and the attitude that make a vacation an enjoyable experience. Let's explore how to make a fun family vacation happen.

Wise Planning

Plan, but don't overschedule. There is a healthy balance. Do the research ahead of time to find out what is worth doing, seeing, and visiting at your destination. As much as humanly possible, keep the activities age-appropriate. (Don't drag a three-year-old to an ancient artifacts museum, and avoid taking a teenager to a children's playground.) Do your homework via books, magazines, friends, and the Internet. More important, as your kids get older, assign the research to them. This will build their excitement about the trip and help them take ownership of the experience.

Using your research, create a list of opportunities, activities, and interests that you can experience on the trip. Have each family member circle one or two activities on the list that they especially want to do. Instead of scheduling every moment of each day, consider going over your list each morning during breakfast and choosing one or two activities to do that day. This system helps you plan around the weather for that day and takes into account how family members are feeling physically (tired, energetic, sickly).

Plan your destination carefully. I've interviewed many families for this chapter and have heard the good, the bad, and the ugly about family vacations. Two suggestions (or perhaps I should call them warnings) surfaced in my discussions. One was "Don't take five kids, stuff them in a car with nothing to do, and drive nonstop for six hours." This is a prescription for misery for both parents and children, whether you are traveling via car or plane. The other suggestion was "If you have a wide variance of ages in the family, try to go to a place that has a little something for everyone." Let's tackle both of these warnings with a positive plan.

Make Travel Time Enjoyable

Prepare a travel goody bag for each child. Perhaps the most effective way to make travel time a success (whether you are on the road or in the air) is to prepare a travel goody bag for each child. This can be a simple bag of goodies that you hand the kids right before you begin the journey. Customize the bags to your child's interests and age. You will want to include a snack and a small drink, a simple game or book, colored pencils or markers, a journal or coloring book or puzzle book, and perhaps a small toy. For older kids, you may want to give them a favorite CD for their player *with earphones!*

Plan to stop along the way. Do a little research to find out a good restaurant or park or place of interest along the route. When it comes to kids, your trip will be much more enjoyable if you offer them a few bathroom breaks as well as a chance to stretch their legs. Certain auto clubs such as AAA (www.aaa.com/stop) will help you plan a trip.

Add some entertainment. Many families now take their portable DVD player or laptop in the car to watch movies the entire way. I do think movies help the trip go much faster and make the traveling much more enjoyable. You also may want to include a book on tape or CD. But I also want to encourage you to leave some room for interaction or to talk about the trip itself. One fond memory that I have is of my mother reading a passage of the Bible to us during car trips. For younger kids, you can have a story hour or even bring along a puppet for entertainment.

Play a few travel games. Stimulate the brain and add some family interaction with good ol' travel games. Here are a few to consider:

- *ABC Adventure.* One family member begins by saying something like, "I'm Anne. I'm driving in an automobile, and I'm going to Alabama." The next person says a name that starts with a B (such as Brittany), traveling in something that starts with a B (such as a boat), and going to a destination that starts with a B (such as Bermuda). And so on throughout the alphabet.
- *I Spy (Magazine Version).* Before the trip, tear out pictures from magazines of objects you could possibly see out of the window as you travel (barns, houses, cows, people, planes). Find three or four per family member. Place the pictures facedown and allow each person to take several. When the driver says go, everyone looks at his or her pictures. The first person to spy objects that match each of the pictures wins. You can then scramble the pictures and play again.
- *20 Questions.* You start off saying, "I'm thinking of a place." A family member responds, "Is it in America?" Each question demands only a yes or no response. If you make it through twenty questions and no one has guessed what you are thinking of, then you win. If someone guesses wrong, they are out. If someone guesses correctly before twenty questions are asked, they become the winner and start a new round. You can begin with a person, place, or thing.
- *Car Trip Sing-Along.* You may want to bring a sing-along tape, or if you are musically talented, then you can do it yourself. Start with some of the kids' favorites. Add familiar songs from church, camp songs, and patriotic

songs. My favorites are "Do Your Ears Hang Low?" "This Little Light of Mine," and "I've Got That Joy, Joy, Joy, Joy Down in My Heart." Of course, "99 Bottles of Anything" is not allowed to be sung in our car because we want to maintain our sanity!

Plan Destinations Where There Is Something for Everyone

In my family, we have two girls, one year apart in age. It's easy to entertain both with the same type of agenda and activities. Not so with a family of three kids ranging in age from fourteen to five. In the case of a wide span of ages and different genders, you can find some happy compromises. Here are a few suggestions from families that found a happy haven for all:

- The beach
- Dude ranch
- Family camp
- The mountains

Family togetherness activities for a range of ages include these:

- Hiking
- Cooking a meal together if you have a kitchen
- Swimming
- Walking on the beach
- Horseback riding or biking
- Puzzles and board games
- Sea World, aquariums, zoos
- Picnics
- Some museums and monuments
- Amusement parks that offer something for everyone
- Water parks
- Boat rides

Flexibility

Every spring break we go to Destin, Florida. Our kids' spring break comes earlier than most, so we typically have a few days of sunshine on the beach and several days of cold and rain. Needless to say, we need to be fairly flexible in what we do. We try to prepare for both possibilities, but it is impossible to know exactly how the week will play out weather-wise. Instead of moping and complaining that our vacation is no fun, we create our own fun.

One of the things we can depend on is change. A change in plans is bound to happen, so we must help our family understand the importance of adjusting. It helps to take a short moment to acknowledge the disappointment. ("Oh, I'm so sorry this didn't work out. I know you are disappointed.") Then begin forming a new plan together. This is a good opportunity to hone everyone's ingenuity and problem-solving skills. Here are a few ideas to consider:

In case of bad weather:

- Check out local indoor amusements, museums, and shopping.
- Visit a bookstore, give everyone a certain amount of money, and have them find their own treasure to read.
- Go to a craft store and pick out one craft to do together or individual crafts for everyone.
- Go get ice cream or milk shakes.
- Have a family uplift meeting. Write down or tell all the qualities you admire about each family member. You may want to choose one family member each day whom you will bless with encouraging words.
- Complete a puzzle together.
- Go to a movie or rent a movie.

- If you have a kitchen, bake something together, such as cookies or a pizza.
- Purchase a new board game and play as a family.

In case of being stuck at an airport (layover, flight cancellation, etc.):

- Play card games.
- Play I Spy or some of the travel games listed above.
- Observe people; guess their occupation and destination.
- Watch a movie on your laptop.
- Give each other back rubs.
- Draw pictures with your fingers on the kids' backs. See if they can guess what you drew.
- Read a book to the kids.
- Buy a newspaper for each child and have a scavenger hunt (find the comics, a high school sports score, a political editorial, a picture of a star, and an advice column).

A Good Attitude

It may sound trite, but the best thing you can pack for your family vacation is a good attitude. Before your trip begins, it is important to talk about the importance of choosing to be pleasant during the trip. Whining will not be tolerated. If the kids have a request or complaint, they can share it respectfully (as we learned in chapter 2), but they may not whine or complain. You may even want to demonstrate the difference between the two.

One friend gives her kids spending money for each trip, but if they whine or complain, they have to give her back a dollar. I love that idea! You can imagine it only takes one whining episode for the kids to see that Mom means business, and they don't like having their spending money diminished. You may find it fun to have a silly symbol that you will make if someone is whining. My husband used to act as if he was playing a violin when I complained about anything. He said it was the world's smallest violin playing "My Heart Bleeds for You." It always made me laugh and certainly curbed the whining.

Encourage your kids, if they don't like an activity or situation, to try to think of something they can be thankful for in it (just like the Glad Game from *Pollyanna*). You may even want to have a reward system for every time your kids smile or say something with a grateful spirit. One time I made my teenagers memorize Philippians 4:11 before a trip. It says, "I have learned to be content whatever the circumstances." All I had to say was "4-11" and they got the message. We can teach our kids (as well as ourselves) to look for the good, ignore the bad, and work through the challenges.

My Vacation Heroes

When I think of savvy travelers, I look to my sister and her family. She and her husband, David, are the primo vacation planners. I listen in awe as they tell me about their family adventures both near and far. Now mind you, my sister is a former accountant and one of the most frugal people I know. She is careful to save every penny, and she is careful to make every family trip count. I asked her to share her thoughts about family travel for this chapter. The amazing thing is that I didn't share with her what I was putting into this chapter (the three essential ingredients), but I think you will see it is obvious that we were cut from the same cloth! Here are some travel tips from the expert, my sis, Karen Smith.

Our family loves to travel. We make it a priority both time-wise and money-wise. Of course, some of our favorite memories were not the most expensive parts—driving through the mountains in Colorado, climbing on rocks in

Central Park, and eating shaved ice. And some of the short weekend trips have reaped a bounty of fun experiences— exploring caves, wading through clear streams revealing dinosaur fossils, enjoying the forest wonderland on a fall camping trip with cousins, getting pictures made in fields of bluebonnets, and riding in Grandpa's golf cart on family golf trips. If I had to come up with the secret to our most rewarding vacation experiences, I would have to say it is a combination of planning, flexibility, and simply enjoying the people you are spending it with!

Planning ahead may not be everyone's cup of tea, but we actually enjoy it, and there is really no substitute for researching an area that you are going to visit. By handling the bulk of decision making and map studying before the trip instead of during valuable vacation time, we have avoided a lot of aimless wandering—not fun with kids or spouses! It has especially paid off in helping us stay within a budget.

We rent books and videos from the library. My husband looks for deals and coupons online. It also makes for some good conversation with friends. We especially love to go with tips and affirmations from people who know the area and know us! Best of all have been the tips from the Lord above. Indeed, I pray over each trip as part of the planning process and firmly believe that it is God who has blessed us with the smoothness and special "extras" that we have enjoyed.

Of course, exploration and spontaneity can be an important element of any adventure. A favorite trip we took as a couple was a three-day weekend on one of American Airlines' "Wednesday Specials." You could get an incredibly cheap fare if you chose a city listed on Wednesday to fly to that weekend. So we decided to just pick a weekend to get away and reserve our babysitter, not knowing where we would be going! What a rush to see LA on the list when it appeared on our computer screen at 5:00 a.m. that Wednesday! It was great fun, but of course, most trips could not be enjoyed that way—especially with kids.

As important as planning is, however, many happy memories were truly born of flexibility. I don't just mean staying open to some plan B options, but really having a humble attitude toward the expectations and needs of the rest of my family. We had been having a great week in Boston, and it was time to head back home. We had a flight situation arise which meant a long delay, so we decided it made more sense to stay an extra day. Well, thanks to the flexibility of my husband, who swallowed his skepticism about the "guarantee" of a whale sighting, we splurged and booked a whale-watch that the rest of us had been rooting for. What a trip! We saw lighthouses on the way, and, thank the Lord, we saw more whale tails than we ever imagined and had a rip-roaring time just riding the boat and laughing at one another's Atlantic-windblown hair (mainly mine).

Planning and flexibility have certainly resulted in some great trips for us. Rest assured we have gained some travel savvy over the years. However, no matter what kind of travel experts we think we are, we have come to see that even in an island paradise, the beauty of the surroundings can be overshadowed by hurting hearts if we have focused too much on the trip and not enough on relationships. Certainly if we have allowed selfishness and pride to rule the day, the result will be less than a happy memory. So, as much as we love to plan, we must know that there will always be a hitch or two that will test our focus. Looking back, it is easy to see that it was how we responded that had the impact. I have also seen how easily I can set the tone for the way the rest of my family will react.

Our super vacation experiences have been the fruits of prayerful planning, humble flexibility, and enjoying each other. Remember to thank the Lord, by whom you have any and all traveling companions, resources, abilities, and a wonderful creation to explore together![1]

Family Fun Devotional

Read: Proverbs 3:5–6

Talk:

- Who is the ultimate travel director in our lives?
- How does he give us direction?
- What areas in your life do you need to devote to him and trust him with the outcome?

Do:

Get out the calendar and prayerfully plan your next family trip. It may be just one night or several days. It may be in town or out of town, depending on schedule and budget. Carefully plan at least one activity you can enjoy together as a family. There is great joy and anticipation in the planning just as there is in the experiencing.

8

Keeping Your Sanity While Shopping

Hold tight rein over three T's—thought, temper, and tongue—and you will have few regrets.

TEEN ESTEEM

It is better to be patient than powerful; it is better to have self-control than to conquer a city.

PROVERBS 16:32 NLT

Has it ever occurred to you that the only time in Scripture when Jesus lost his temper was with the buyers, sellers, and money changers? Of course, our little outbursts can't always be attributed to "righteous indignation," but shopping with kids typically is a tension-filled time. Whether we are juggling two preschoolers while shopping for groceries or hunting for something "decent to wear" with several teenagers, tempers can flare quite easily.

As much shopping as we do with the kids in tow, you would think that we could eventually achieve victory in keeping our sanity while shopping. The problem is, just when we figure out how to keep the kids entertained during a shopping excursion, they grow into a new phase and their interests change. We must adjust and flex in order to keep the peace with the pace. I believe that with a few thoughtful adjustments to our normal shopping routine, we can create an enjoyable family shopping experience.

We can handle some of the potential shopping challenges proactively by taking preventive measures before we leave the house. We also want to be equipped with some quick and creative ways to deal with difficulties on the spot when they do arise. In this chapter, we will explore creative ways to make shopping a more positive experience for both you and your kids.

Preventive Measures

Shopping success begins by being prepared and taking precautions. Consider the following checklist before setting out for a shopping adventure. It may take a few extra moments before you leave, but the end result will be a good experience with fewer complaints.

- Are the kids (and you) well rested? Tired often equals temper tantrums.
- Have the kids been fed? Don't take a hungry child shopping unless you plan to feed him there.
- Visit the bathroom before you begin.
- In a positive tone, tell your kids where you are taking them and what you expect of their behavior. Caryl Waller Krueger, in her book *1001 Things to Do with Your Kids*, suggests the big three grocery shopping rules: walk, talk, and gawk. Walk, but no running or pushing permitted. Talk, but no crying or shouting allowed. Gawk (or look), but don't pester for things.[1]
- Make your list of what you need before you go. You can speed up the shopping if you write what you will need in each section of the store. You may find it helpful to create a master list of your most commonly bought

items. Print copies so you can simply circle the ones you need for the present week.

- Instruct the kids on what they can purchase or choose within the budget.
- Pack what you need. A toddler may need a toy in hand to keep his attention while you shop. A bottle or extra diapers can prevent a shopping trip from turning into a disaster.
- Consider shopping online for certain products and clothing.
- Choose kid-friendly stores and malls. Fun grocery baskets, safe play areas, and the availability of kid food can make a lot of difference in your experience.

Shopping Can Be Fun

Yes, it is possible to make the shopping experience a fun time for both you and the kids. Here are a few ideas for a variety of ages.

Babies

Teething Toys. Bring along at least one or two teething toys to use if your baby becomes fussy. You may want to use a ribbon to tie it to the basket so it won't drop (or be thrown) on the floor.

Sleeping Babies. For a young baby who sleeps soundly, time your shopping so he can sleep through the ride in the cart.

Front Carrier or Sling. If your baby does best by being held, then consider bringing along a sling or front carrier so your hands can be free while your baby feels your closeness and warmth.

Preschoolers

Busy Hands. Busy hands are happy hands. Bring a small toy or book to keep your child's interest. You can also give your child an assignment to help you, such as holding your coupons (if he won't destroy them—you know your child), looking for an item on the shelf, or holding certain safe items.

Learn and Shop. Engage little ones in the shopping experience and create a learning opportunity as well. For instance, help your kids learn colors by saying, "Mommy is looking for the green jar. Can you point to the green jar? Yes! That's it!" "Now Mommy needs the blue box. Can you show me which one is blue?" Encourage the kids to help you count the apples or the cans of soft drinks.

Positive Motivation. You can call it bribery if you want, but I am not above offering my children a simple motivator if they maintain a good attitude or don't fight during grocery-shopping time. The reward should be simple: their favorite movie after nap-time, snuggle time with Mommy during reading time, calling Daddy to tell him what a good job they did, special playtime when they get home, etc. Make the reward clear before you set out to shop. You don't want your children to get the impression that if they are bad enough, they can motivate you to offer a reward.

Containment. If possible, bring the stroller or double stroller into the store to help the kids have their place instead of wide-open space for running.

Older Kids

Divide and Conquer. Give each child a list of several things you need. Tell them to meet you in the front of the store in a certain amount of time. Be sure it is a safe environment before sending kids off by themselves. Send them in groups if possible.

Coupon Accountant. Perhaps one of your kids has an accountant-type aptitude. Assign him or her to be in charge of clipping coupons each week, organizing them, and helping you use them accordingly.

Meal Planning. Allow each of your older children to plan one meal that they would like during the week. Tell them to write down the ingredients they will need (encourage them to look up the recipe). When they are at the grocery store with you, they can find the things on their list for their favorite meal.

Push, Bag, and Unload. Older kids can feel useful by pushing the cart for you and helping the checker bag the groceries. They can also help hand items to you if you are doing self-checkout. Loading the groceries into the car and unloading the groceries at home can also help the kids feel a sense of responsibility.

Meltdown on Aisle Seven

You've made your list, packed toys and a bottle for the baby, fed the kids before you left, and even planned a fun activity, but it still happens. Your toddler throws a major tantrum because he wants the cereal with an action figure on the front of the box, even though you know he will never eat the stuff. Now you are faced with a choice. You could scream and yell at him, give in to his pleas, negotiate a compromise, punish him, or simply leave the store.

Often the most difficult part of a temper tantrum is the scene it creates and the glares it brings from bystanders. We are afraid most of them are thinking, *What that kid needs is a good, strict dose of discipline.* That sounds well and good, but it isn't always easy to administer discipline at the store, especially when you know that there is a strong potential for louder and more vibrant screaming (your child's, not yours).

So how do you handle the infamous temper tantrum in the middle of the store?

Stay calm. Experts agree that as you manage your own anger and demonstrate self-control, you offer stability and a good role model to help your child get it back together. Take a few deep breaths to relax your body physically and provide a moment to gain your composure.

Recognize this is not personal. Your child is not doing this with the intention of humiliating you in front of the entire store (although you may feel that way). Typically a child who is throwing a tantrum is frustrated and needs authority, comfort, and/or help.

Distract your child. Get your child to focus on something else. Draw his attention away from the point of frustration, and give him something he can hold and play with or focus on.

Hold your child. This works with some children and is not the best approach with others. One of my daughters needed to be held during a fit, while my other daughter writhed and bent back in anger if I tried to hold her. Most kids under two years of age are not able to verbalize what they want, so a gentle embrace when they are out of control can help them feel a sense of security and calm. Don't forcefully hold your child.

Ignore some tantrums. There are times when kids may throw a fit just to get your attention. If you sense this is the case, then ignoring it can be a wise remedy. If possible, start walking in the other direction and let them see it is not working.

Remove yourself and the child from the immediate source of frustration. If the cereal box is the tantrum source, then move down the aisle or to the next row as soon as possible. If you are in the checkout lane (a common place for end-of-shopping-trip tantrum), try to make any change in direction or location possible (move to the bagging station at the end of the lane or turn the cart around so your child is facing a different direction).

Communicate. Toddlers especially have trouble communicating what they want, so they throw a tantrum to get the point across. Identify what is frustrating your child and verbalize it. "I know you are angry (sad, frustrated)." Older kids often need to know you understand, so you could say, "I understand you are frustrated that you can't have that magazine. It's not appropriate for your age, so choose a different one." Make sure your words are respectful, kind, and firm.

Don't try to reason with a screaming kid. Wait until your child calms down and gains composure. If you maintain this pattern, your child will learn that when he or she is reasonable, you are willing to listen. When your child is ranting and raving, he or she has no say-so. Please see proper ways to negotiate or register a complaint in chapter 2.

Keep your word. If you said no, stick with it. If you eventually give in, you will give your kids the signal of tantrum victory, and they have learned that if they fuss long enough and loud enough, they will get what they want.

Know your child. Try to diffuse a tantrum before it gets started or goes too far. As an attentive parent, you can begin to recognize the signs before the storm, such as an agitated spirit or body language. Use gentle words and eye contact to let them know you are aware of their struggle.

Shopping with Teens

Two shopping issues that seem to surface during the teenage years are the areas of how much our teens can spend and what clothes they are allowed to wear. Again, creative preparation on your part can make the difference between a positive shopping experience and a negative one. Let's take a practical look at both.

How Much Teens Can Spend

As the teen years approach, it is a good idea to form a budget. Every household is different as to what they can afford and what they want to spend. Just because you have the money doesn't mean you need to spend it. It is healthy and good for our kids to learn restraint and to work under a budget in order to gain a sense of financial responsibility. During the middle school years, you may want to create a system of spending that works for your family. Here are a few possibilities:

Clothing Allowance. Each month, your teenager is given a designated amount to spend on clothing. You will need to decide if this includes shoes and underwear or if you will buy those for them. The clothing allowance has several benefits. Kids begin to learn the value of a dollar as compared to the value of a label. If they just "have" to have those designer jeans (which takes up all of their allowance for the next two months), then they will begin to understand budgeting and worth. How much should you give a teen? I'm truly sorry that I cannot answer that question for you. You may find it helpful to discuss with other parents of teens what is reasonable.

Seasonal Shopping Trips. Choose four to six times a year when you will go shopping together with a budgeted amount of money for that trip. Again you will need to predetermine the amount per trip and also what to do with the money that is not spent. (Will it be deferred to the next shopping trip?) Possible shopping times could include back to school, fall, winter/Christmas, springtime, and beginning of summer.

Work to Buy. In this approach, your teens earn their own money (or half the money) for their clothes. This puts them in the driver's seat as far as how much they want to earn and spend on clothes. For younger teens who are not old enough to get a paying job outside the home, you can set up a chore system in which they earn a certain amount for their work. Of course, there are jobs such as babysitting, raking leaves, yardwork, and pet sitting that young teens can also do outside the home.

What Teens Are Allowed to Wear

Now the dilemma of what they are allowed to wear. There is a healthy balance between kids being able to express some of their personality through what they wear and wearing what is decent, appropriate, and respectful. Often (but not always), clothes are a reflection of what is going on in the heart. If there is rebellion in the heart, it may be expressed in the choice of clothing and jewelry. And then, of course, the obvious—a girl who is desperate for male attention will tend to dress immodestly.

So how do you appeal to the heart? Don't wait until you are at the shopping mall or clothing store to have these discussions. Here are some thoughts on how to build a good understanding between you and your teen when it comes to clothes:

Look at a few current magazines together. Discuss why people wear what they wear and what it says about them. Talk about how, like it or not, people do evaluate others by what they wear. Ask your son or daughter what image or message they want to portray through what they wear.

Looks at a few catalogs to get a feel for what is being offered at some of your favorite stores. This is also an opportunity to compare prices and figure out what stores give you the best value for your money.

Discuss boundaries. There may be one or two things (keep it minimal) that you don't want your kids to wear. Tell them exactly why you feel that particular type of clothing is inappropriate. Let them know you respect their opinions and listen to them, but also let them know that they represent your family and there are certain lines that should not be crossed.

Remember different tastes. Keep in mind that your child not only is in a different generation and is quite a bit younger but also has a different personality than you do. Please give room for teens to express their personalities; don't demand that they fit your tastes. As long as they are staying within your discussed boundaries, then allow your teenagers some freedom even though you think their clothing choices look ugly.

Help your child distinguish needs from wants. Before going to the store, make a list of what you need to get and then a list of wants if you have money left over in the budget.

Stay quiet. As much as possible, allow your kids to shop according to their tastes without giving your opinion. Fewer words are better when it comes to giving your opinion on a shopping trip.

Family Fun Devotional

Read: Colossians 3:12–15

Talk:

- Describe the clothing Paul says we should wear as Christians.
- What did he say was the most important piece of clothing?
- What kind of effect do these clothes have on others?

Do:

Grab some old T-shirts you have around the house or buy a package of men's T-shirts (one for each member of the family). Decide together how you want to decorate the shirts with the words from Colossians. You may want to use scraps of cloth, paint, or permanent markers. Write the words or create picture symbols to represent the different qualities. You may want to read Colossians 3:5–10 and talk about some qualities that need to be thrown out.

9

Five Ingredients for Enjoying a Delightful Meal

Sitting down at a dinner table with your children is one of the most important things you can do for your family.

GWEN ELLIS

Better is a dinner of herbs where love is than a fatted ox and hatred with it.

PROVERBS 15:17 AMP

How would you describe the perfect family dinner? Would it be a delicious, home-cooked meal that suits everyone's taste? Should it include a lovely centerpiece and perfectly appointed place settings? What about well-dressed, well-mannered family members who arrive at the dinner table on time without having to be called?

Right now you are probably thinking, *If that's what I have to do to have a great family dinner, then forget it! Sounds nice, but it won't happen at my house.* Never fear! A delightful meal with kids and hubby doesn't have to look like a picture out of Martha Stewart's *Living*. In fact, personally speaking, if I tried to accomplish all of the criteria above, it may look good on the outside, but I would be a frazzled, short-tempered mess on the inside.

Thankfully, positive and enriching family meals are doable for regular people like you and me.

Most of us recognize that in our culture today, the typical family dinner hour is dying a fast death, yet dinnertime is a vital time for developing relationships. A study done by the National Center on Addiction and Substance Abuse at Columbia University revealed that frequent family dinners cut teens' substance abuse risk in half. "The more often children and teens eat dinner with their families, the less likely they are to smoke, drink and use drugs."[1] The study goes on to say that children and teens who participate in frequent family dinners

- are less likely to have friends or classmates who use illicit drugs or abuse prescription drugs;
- have lower levels of tension and stress at home;
- are more likely to say that their parents are proud of them;
- are more likely to say they can confide in their parents;
- are more likely to get better grades in school;
- are more likely to be emotionally content and have positive peer relationships;
- have healthier eating habits;
- are at lower risk for thoughts of suicide.[2]

Wow! If you were uncertain of the importance of family dinners, I bet you have a stronger opinion now. Family dinners have a long-term, positive impact on our kids. In this chapter, I want to inspire and equip you with ideas for how to create meaningful and fun dinnertimes for your family. Don't feel guilty if you can't do family dinners every night. Do what you can, and try to make it a priority.

My hope is that as you delight in planning dinner, your joy will spread to the rest of your family. Let me assure you that you don't have to cook elaborate meals or make everything look perfect. Solomon said, "A dry crust eaten in peace is better than a great feast with strife" (Proverbs 17:1 NLT). A great attitude and a little food go a long way in feeding one's body, mind, and soul.

The five key ingredients for making dinnertime a delight are simple preparation, great conversation, a respectful attitude, fun flair, and family participation.

Simple Preparation

The hour before dinner for most of us could be called "the killer hour." Everyone is hungry. The baby is fussy, the kids are restless, Dad is weary, and Mom is frazzled. After-school activities, homework, and errands seem to pull us in a million different directions. Needless to say, preparation for dinner for many of us must be minimal by sheer necessity. There may be days when it is easier to cook and eat at home, then there may be days when the best you can do is drive through.

Here are some tips to help you through the dinner hour with simple preparation so that you can enjoy your dinner together.

Quick and Easy Recipes

Personally, I look for recipes that have five or fewer ingredients and very little chopping required. There are several cookbooks that I have found helpful, which I have listed in the resource section at the back of the book. My best source for good, family-friendly recipes is my friends. We share what works and what doesn't. Here are three of my easiest dinners that I want to share with you:

- *Crock-Pot Roast:* 5 to 6 lb. beef rump roast, one packet of dry onion soup mix, one can of cream of mushroom soup, one cup of water, and salt and pepper. Dump it all in the

Crock-Pot in the morning. Let it slow cook all day. Add vegetables or potatoes if you like. Serve with bread (prepared garlic bread is great) and a salad (out of the bag, of course), and you have one great, easy-to-prepare, home-cooked meal (that makes the house smell good too).

- *Spiral-Cut Honey Baked Ham:* Look for them on sale after the holidays at your local grocery. One ham can go a long way. Heat it up for dinner, along with baked sweet potatoes (wrap in foil and bake at 350 degrees for 40 minutes) and tossed salad (add dried cranberries, pecans, and feta cheese along with your favorite dressing). Use leftovers for breakfast, or mac and cheese with ham, or ham sandwiches, or club salad—and don't forget to make bean soup with the ham bone.

- *Roasted Chicken:* Many grocery stores sell prepared rotisserie chicken fully cooked, which is a wonderful help. You can also buy a whole chicken and stuff it with a whole, peeled onion. Rub it with butter and season it with salt, pepper, and rosemary. Cover and bake at 350 degrees for 1 to 1½ hours or until fully cooked. Serve with biscuits, favorite veggies, and sliced oranges. You can boil the remains (straining out the bones) to make chicken broth for chicken noodle soup later in the week.

You may also want to consider what I call "partial drive-through" as an option. I have found that when I am toting kids here and there after school, I may need the help of a local drive-through for at least part of the meal. Bring home a bucket of fried chicken, serve with veggies or fruit you already have at home, and everyone is pleased. In purchasing fast food and bringing it home, I can still maintain dinnertime with family while having a little relief from the preparation.

Serve dinner with a KISS (keep it smart and simple). One of

my husband's favorite meals is a patty melt. Yes, it is simply a grilled hamburger patty with cheese and a sliced onion on top. Whenever I grill the patty melt for him, I offer hamburger tacos to my daughters. All I do is chop up a patty melt and serve it in soft tortillas. They love it and think I'm some sort of great cook! Chicken breast baked in Italian dressing has gotten me out of a lot of fixes as well. And never underestimate the blessing of having a frozen pizza or lasagna in the freezer.

The point is to be deliberate about dinner. It does mean giving a little thought and preparation to what you will do. Each Sunday afternoon, consider taking a moment to review the family calendar and make a list of simple and practical dinner plans for each night of the week. You may even want to post "this week's menu" for the whole family to see so they know what they can expect during the week.

Great Conversation

A colorful exchange of ideas during dinnertime not only increases our kids' awareness of issues and ideas but also improves their social skills. How do we get good, healthy chats under way? It's a good idea to have an arsenal of ideas and conversation starters. You may want to consider a different topic or theme for discussion each night of the week. For instance:

- Sunday night—Church or theological issues
- Monday night—Sports and hobbies
- Tuesday night—School-related issues
- Wednesday night—Friendships and relationships
- Thursday night—Current events
- Friday night—Entertainment (latest movies, music, books)
- Saturday night—True stories (about missionaries, heroes, people in the news)

You can use these topics to help lead your conversation. For instance, on Monday night you may talk about your favorite football game from the weekend and who you think will win on Monday night. On Wednesday night you may want to ask about some of the qualities the kids like in their friends, or whether they have any new friendships that seem to be growing. On Thursday night you may talk about something that is happening in the national news or maybe in the news in your area of town. Topics help you have a direction in which to take conversation so that you are not asking the same old "What did you do today?"

Here are some additional ways to get conversation started:

The Question Box. Sit down with some friends and create a list of interesting, open-ended questions. Make some of them funny and some of them deep. Write each question down on an index card and put it in a shoe box. You may even want to decorate the box. Once a week at dinner, pull out the question box and allow one person to reach in and pull out a question. Then go around the table and allow everyone to answer it.

Candy-Coated Questions. Purchase a small bag of assorted colored candies (such as M&M's, Starburst, lollipops). To prepare for this game, you will need to write a different question for each color. For instance:

- Blue—What is your favorite movie and why?
- Green—Where would you like to take your dream vacation?
- Red—If you found a twenty-dollar bill in your pocket that you didn't realize you had, what would you do with it?

As family members pick a candy out of the bag, they answer the question that correlates to the color they drew. You can go around several times with this game, as I'm sure your kids won't mind drawing a new piece of candy out of the bag. You may want them to set the candy aside to save it for dessert.

Ask Another. Write each family member's name on a piece of paper. Randomly put one paper under each dinner plate (or you can tape it under the chair). When you are ready, have each person look at the name they received, and then one by one they must ask their given person a question. You may have a pool of several questions to choose from, or each person may come up with one on their own.

Conversation-Starter Questions

Here are a few questions to get you started in family conversation. You will need to simplify the questions for young people, so at the end I have added a few questions for the little ones.

- If you could start a restaurant, what would it be called and what would be on the menu?
- If you could donate a million dollars to the charities of your choice, to what groups or organizations would you give?
- If you could take one friend and go on a one-week, all-expenses-paid vacation, where would you go and who would you bring?
- If you were going to make a movie, who would star in it and what would it be about?
- What would be the title of your autobiography, and what would be some of the highlights?
- Where in this world do you want to visit before you die?
- Describe your dream dinner and who you would invite.
- If you could go back in history, what era or time period would you choose and why?
- If you could be one Bible character, who would you be?

- If you had to perform one talent on stage in front of an audience, what would it be?
- If you had two days to go away and relax from all responsibilities, what would you do?

Questions for little ones:

- Who is your favorite Bible character?
- Where is your favorite place to visit?
- What animal do you like best?
- Which books do you like to read?
- What do you like to draw?
- Which color is your favorite?
- Which room do you like best in our house?
- Where is your favorite place to play?
- What is your favorite toy?

Take a look at the resources section at the back of the book for some great books specifically focused on conversation starters around the dinner table or even when you are out at a restaurant. Keep your conversation positive and uplifting. Don't use dinnertime as a time to confront or reprimand your kids for something that has been brewing during the day. Certainly maintain respect and order, but keep the conversation upbeat.

A Respectful Attitude

A respectful attitude and manners set the tone for a pleasant meal. The dinner table is not the place for whining, complaining, or arguing. While our kids are young, we want to gradually and consistently teach them some of the rules of respect at the dinner table. Don't overwhelm your kids with too many rules or manners. Keep your expectations age-appropriate and easy to follow.

Here are some points to teach:

- No frowns, rolling of the eyes, or ugly faces will be permitted at the dinner table.
- If you don't think you will like the food, try at least a few bites; it won't kill you.
- Do not make any negative comments about the food.
- Always use the words *please* and *thank you.* One parent I know says, "I didn't hear you," if the kids do not say please or thank you.
- Eye contact is necessary during conversations.
- Do not interrupt someone else who is talking.
- Do not reach across another person. Instead, ask, "Would you please pass the butter?"
- Stay at the table until you are excused. For older children, you may want to teach them to ask to be excused. For example, "May I please be excused?" Parents, be reasonable and understanding of age. It is very difficult for a toddler to sit for long periods of time, so this is a rule to gradually work into.
- Speak with a gentle and kind tone.

Remember, the best way for your kids to learn good manners and respectful conversation is to see them modeled by you. Make sure you are showing the proper care for others through your own display of kindness. Politeness and consideration of others are your end goals, but these don't happen overnight. It takes time and gentle training to get there. Be patient yet consistent, and you will eventually see good results.

Fun Flair

With a little thought, you can add some flair to your normal mealtime routine. Here are some easy tips for putting a little pizzazz into your family dinners.

Manners Night. Once a month, declare a manners night. Ask all family members to dress nicely. You could hand out invitations if you want to go the extra mile. Serve dinner on the fine china and nice tablecloth. Teach one or two rules of etiquette at the dinner table, and talk about the importance of respecting one another.

Dinner Theme. Every once in a while, build a theme around your dinner. On Mexican night, decorate the table with bright colors and a sombrero for tacos and tamales. On Italian night, use a red-checked tablecloth as you serve spaghetti. Of course, Valentine's dinner can be red foods with paper hearts. On St. Patrick's Day serve a green dinner (with the help of food coloring) on a green tablecloth with paper shamrocks scattered on the table.

Seasonal Celebration. At the beginning of each season, celebrate with a related dinner. The beginning of winter can be celebrated with paper snowflakes and snowball ice cream for dessert (roll vanilla ice cream in coconut). For the first day of spring, place fresh flowers on the table (or make tissue-paper flowers) and serve cookies shaped like flowers for dessert.

Kids' Cooking Night. Allow older kids to search the recipe books and plan their favorite menu. They will need to make a list for you ahead of time so you can get the ingredients at the store. Then allow them to cook the meal, with only a little guidance from you if they need it. It is also their job to set the table. This activity tends to give them a greater appreciation for what you do.

Place Mat Art. Allow kids to make different place mats each year. Using a large piece of colored construction paper, they can draw or color, make a collage, paint a scene, or use photos. You can even take an old map of the United States and cut it down to make place mats. Take the completed mats to an office or teacher supply store to get them laminated, or use clear contact paper to do it yourself. Keep the collection of mats over the years and bring them out now and then. It's fun to see the progression of your children's talents and abilities.

Family Participation

When it comes to dinnertime, everyone can do a little something. Some families create chore charts with various responsibilities. Honestly, I was never a chart person. I often created chore charts (and made them up all cute and fun), but then I always forgot about them after a few weeks. There's my true confession. For me, it was easier to simply give my daughters different responsibilities each week. One set the table, while the other had the responsibility of cleaning it up. Then the next week we switched.

Make it work for your family. You can read a dozen books to get ideas, but when it comes down to it, you know your family best. Find a plan that works for you and won't frustrate you when it comes to family participation. You may want to solicit help in the areas of unloading the dishwasher, making a salad, pouring the drinks, calling everyone to dinner, or helping to stir and cook. If everyone pitches in with help in some form or fashion, they will take a little more pride in the meal and there may be less complaining!

The point is to make your dinners a positive experience that will enhance your sense of family and build connectedness among the members. I want to close this chapter with a poem written by a talented young father who recognizes the challenges and the importance of family dinnertimes.

Dinner Time
by Sammy Young

Quadruple tasking, sweat glistening on your brow
with a fresh burn draped in ice wrapped in a towel
and not a "May I help?" comes from the inner
but a hungry voice yelling "What's for dinner?"
So why then do you smile instead of frown?
Because you know your efforts will bring forth crowns.

It's dinner time with family and no other place
can give you teaching and loving and warm embrace.
All the "He's kicking me's" and "Eat your beans" yes, it's
    a hassle
but you're doing more than eating, you're building a castle.
One that is strong and firm and impenetrable from evil
    forces
One that comes not from stone or mortar but love from
    voices.[3]

Family Fun Devotional

Read: 1 Corinthians 10:31

Talk:

- How can we honor the Lord in what we eat and drink?
- What are some ways people may dishonor the Lord in what they eat or drink?
- Why do we say grace or pray before a meal?

Do:

Family Cooking Night

Decide on a dinner menu and divide up the responsibilities so that one person is preparing the salad, another the main course, another the dessert, and so on. Have a wonderful time laughing and hanging out together. As you eat the meal, choose one of the conversation-starter games in this chapter to do while you eat.

10

Reaching Out in Compassion

I am a little pencil in the hand of a writing God who is sending a love letter to the world.

MOTHER TERESA

Little children, let us not love with word or with tongue, but in deed and truth.

1 JOHN 3:18 NASB

Sara has a heart of compassion and the gift of mercy. Whenever there is a need in the church or community, Sara immediately has a plan to help. From feeding the homeless to ministering to cancer patients to serving dinners to the Katrina evacuees, Sara wants to serve behind the scenes to bless others. The beautiful thing is, her daughters have a heart for the hurting as well, and that's no accident. Compassion is not genetic, but it is magnetic. The best way to teach the next generation how to care for the needs of others is for them to learn from our own actions.

Serving together not only generates compassion but also builds sweet memories and bonds you together as a family. As your family serves together, you will have moments of laughter and moments of tears, but you will also view life a little differently. When we reach out to help another in need, our problems and complaints tend to look a little smaller. There is no better cure for whining than to visit a place filled with people who have desperate and immediate needs.

Follow Your Heart

How do you know where to serve? Where do you begin to find the needs? I believe God puts in each of us a certain care and concern for specific needs. Personally, I love special-needs kids, so for me the Special Olympics or Disability Resources offers a heartfelt opportunity to serve. My daughter Grace feels called to minister to the homeless, not only with food but with care, compassion, and a listening ear. She loves visiting the homeless in our city and talking with them, giving them encouragement and hope.

Not to say that we should only minister within our favorite area or comfort zone, but I do think that we can begin our journey of compassion by taking a step in the direction of interest God has placed in our hearts. Sometimes it is that first step that is the hardest. I want to encourage you to take some time alone with God and ask him to show you the direction you should go to reach out to others. Ask him for courage and wisdom to take that first step in doing something.

Doors of opportunity are open in many different areas. Certainly your home church is a good place to start in order to discover ministry and service opportunities. You may also want to contact volunteer services at a local hospital, nursing home, or community center. After-school tutoring programs, Meals on Wheels, and local food pantries always need volunteers of all ages.

Create a list of several options you can do as a family. Sit down over dinner and discuss what you want to pursue together. Pray as a family and ask the Lord to direct you in what you should do and how you can best minister to others. Set a date to carry out the plan. You may not be able to do everything, but you can do something and you will be blessed in the process.

Here are several stories of families who have found the joy of service together. I hope you will find their adventures both a blessing and an inspiration.

Serving Meals at a Homeless Shelter

Several years ago, the Reppert family decided to step out of their comfort zone during the holidays and reach out as a family to touch someone else. They decided to take their three kids (ages seventeen, thirteen, and eight) to serve Thanksgiving dinner to the occupants of a homeless shelter in downtown Dallas. Their job was to go around to the tables and serve food to the men, women, and children. There were all ages and stages of people—some families, some singles.

More important than the food, the Repperts offered smiles, love, and a listening ear. Amy (the mom) reflected on the experience: "It was a blessing to ask them, 'How was your meal? Would you like a dessert?' or 'May I get you anything else?' knowing that they were rarely asked these questions." She added, "It felt like we were giving them back their dignity." What a beautiful gift to give!

There were some moments of laughter together as well. When the Repperts arrived, they were told they would have to put on hairnets and aprons. Not cool for teenage kids! But they all took it in stride, and the humor added to the family experience.

When the Repperts returned to their car, they exchanged the names and stories of those they talked to and then prayed for them as a family. Amy summed up the memorable time by telling me, "We all really served! It was neat seeing my kids get in rolling up their sleeves and talking to people they would not have the chance to talk to. Cody [the eight-y

.aking around the desserts and letting the people pick their favorites. I even got to ask a man if he was all right, because it looked like he was crying. I ended up sharing the gospel with him and bringing him a message of hope."

From Here to Romania

The McFarland family has a long history of reaching out to people in need. They help fit kids with new shoes each year during a back-to-school shoe drive with Payless Shoe Stores. They have tirelessly prepared sandwiches, hot dogs, and sack lunches to hand out to the homeless. They have served on their church's missions outreach board. When the opportunity came for them to serve for several weeks with a dental team in Romania, they knew this was the right fit for their family. Dick (the dad) is an orthodontist, and their daughter Lindsay hopes to become an orthodontist one day. Through ServingHIM Healthcare International Ministries, they were able to bring dental supplies and set up a clinic in a village in Romania. Serving together as a family in a foreign country drew them closer as a family and strengthened their character as individuals.

Karen (the mom) recalls one afternoon after a labor-intense day; she was concerned about where her daughters were. She looked out the window and down into the courtyard where the patients waited for their treatment. There she saw a sight she will never forget. Her two daughters (ages nineteen and twenty-one) were sitting with two elderly Romanian women. Their heads were bowed in prayer. After they finished praying, they hugged and cried together, rejoicing over the ladies' newfound faith.

There is nothing more rewarding than to see your daughters grow to love the Lord and serve others together. The McFarland family has had some wonderful trips together, but none as significant as when they worked together helping people and sharing

Christ's love. They have made the journey to Romania twice now and are already making plans for their next visit back.

A New Friendship Is Born

Through the National Charity League, Leslie and her daughters signed up to serve at the Ronald McDonald House in the Dallas area. Their job was to prepare a meal and serve it to the families staying at the house. The Ronald McDonald house provides lodging for out-of-town families while their children are patients at a nearby hospital. One evening while Leslie and her girls and some of their friends were serving dinner at the house, they met Alice.

Alice was twelve years old at the time. She was from Ukraine and was born with many physical limitations and challenges, possibly a result of exposure to radiation from the Chernobyl disaster in Russia. Her neck and spine were not developed, and her legs did not function normally. Her mother, Olga, prayed for her little daughter. Since her daughter obviously would not have a strong body, she asked God if she could have a strong mind. Despite her physical challenges, Alice is extremely intelligent. God answered Olga's prayer. Alice was flown to the United States for extensive surgeries at Children's Medical Center in Dallas, where doctors were able to help straighten her spine and repaired much of the damage in her legs. The Lord has blessed this family with many friends whom they now consider family.

Leslie's family and the other girls immediately befriended this charming young girl in a wheelchair. They grew to know and love her. Leslie and the other moms encouraged Olga as well. The joy of their new friendship grew to the point that they even brought Alice to visit their classmates at school. Alice is now fifteen years old, and the girls still stay in contact. Leslie's family grew from the experience as they reached across physical and cultural differences to see the heart.

Hands Around the World

Another way to reach out from your home is to sponsor a child through one of the organizations that reaches people you may not be able to physically touch. You and your children can take great joy in sponsoring a child. Most sponsorship organizations send you a picture of the person you are sponsoring, which you can use as a reminder to pray for the person. Some organizations encourage you to write the child you are sponsoring as well. Two organizations that you may want to consider are World Vision International (www.wvi.org) and Compassion International (www.compassion.com).

Mission trips are a tremendous way to serve together as a family. Family bonding takes place whenever you travel together, but especially when you serve together in the mission field. Without a doubt, your hearts are knit together in an even deeper way. Mission trips are not just for missionaries. You can take a short-term mission trip in the United States or abroad. Prayerfully consider the type of mission trip that would be a good fit for your family. Check with your church (or other churches in your community) to seek out the possibilities.

You may want to contact one of the following organizations to discover the opportunities available for your family:

- ShortTerm Missions: www.shorttermmissions.com
- ServingHIM Healthcare International Ministries: www.servinghim.org
- International Missions Board: www.imb.org
- Adventures in Missions (AIM): www.adventures.org

Just Serve

As I write this chapter, our nation has just experienced one of the most devastating natural disasters in our history. Hurricane Katrina evacuees have been welcomed with open arms into our city. It was almost overwhelming to think of how to help. So many needs, so many opportunities to serve! So we began to pray, "Lord, where would you have us go, and what would you have us do?"

We couldn't do everything, but we could do something. We found out about a group of people staying at a local La Quinta Inn. Our church made us aware of some of the needs, so we shopped and visited and ministered as a family. It became obvious to me that if each family would reach out and do what they can, much ground would be covered.

In the Bible, we read the story of the little boy who offered his small lunch, and God used his meager offering to bless thousands. You may not be able to serve in big ways right now, but offer God what you do have and what you can do as a family and allow him to do the rest. The point is, just do it. Just serve. Your family will be renewed, strengthened, and blessed in the process.

Here are a few national service organizations you may want to contact:

- Special Olympics: www.specialolympics.org
- Meals on Wheels: www.mowaa.org
- Ronald McDonald House: www.rmhc.com
- Salvation Army: www.salvationarmyusa.org
- Habitat for Humanity: www.habitat.org

Family Fun Devotional

Read: Luke 6:36–38

Talk:

- Why is it important for us to care about other people's needs?
- What are different ways we can give to benefit other people?
- What can we do as a family?

Do:

Prayerfully create a plan to serve together as a family somewhere in your community. Set a date to carry out the plan. After you have served together, talk about your experience. Pray for those people you served, and make a plan to do it again.

step
three

Build Fond Memories

Ah! Memories of sweet summer eves,
Of moonlit wave and willowy way,
Of stars and flowers, and dewy leaves,
And smiles and tones more dear than they!

JOHN GREENLEAF WHITTIER

I recall all you have done, O LORD;
I remember your wonderful deeds of long ago.
They are constantly in my thoughts.
I cannot stop thinking about them.

PSALM 77:11–12 NLT

Fond memories are a gift from God. The joy-filled
activities and celebrations we do with our family today
remain in their hearts for years to come.

11

Grab a Theme and Run with It

The soul without imagination
is what an observatory would be without a telescope.

H. W. Beecher

My heart overflows with a good theme.

Psalm 45:1 NASB

It's summer, and you are at your wit's end, thinking, *What do I do with these kids?* Or maybe you are trying to keep your preschoolers entertained and would love to do something a little more interesting than the normal routine. Then again, you may be dealing with school-age kids who need a little "creative direction" on a Saturday. Finding a good theme could be the perfect solution to a ho-hum day or week.

It's amazing how a simple theme can take a normal day and make it into something memorable or even spectacular. In this chapter, I will give you theme ideas and help spur on your thinking as to what you can do with just a little focus. You can apply these theme ideas in a number of different ways. You may want to use one theme and stretch it out over an entire week, which tends to work best with preschoolers or young kids during the summertime. On the other hand, for the older kids you may choose to create a theme day now and then on a Saturday or during vacation. You will see that this chapter is broken down into different age groups, so you can grab what works best for the kids under your roof.

As you open up a theme, you can open up your door as well. Theme days or theme weeks are loads of fun with cousins and friends. My philosophy is to keep it simple yet centered. You will find that as you center on a theme, excitement and ideas follow. Here are some theme-based activities to get you started and help those creative juices start to flow.

The Preschool Years

Entertaining Royalty

You always knew your kids were little princes and princesses, but now you are going to let them play the part. Here's a way to make your home into a royal palace.

- *Creative Crowns.* Cut crowns out of poster board (or pick up some at Burger King). Decorate with sequins and hobby jewels. For girls, you may want to make a fair lady's hat by spray-painting a little cone party hat and stapling netting material to the top.
- *Dress-Up Clothes.* If you don't already have a dress-up barrel of clothes at your house, now is the time to start one. First, go to your own closet and pull out old formals and dresses that are out of style or you don't wear anymore. Old bridesmaid dresses are perfect. Pull out some of your husband's old shirts or vests (better ask him before you put them in the barrel). You may also want to visit a thrift store for items to fill your barrel. Don't forget to look for costume sales after Halloween.

114

- *Scepters.* Use a cardboard hanger tube or a paper-towel tube for the scepter. You can then stick or glue a Styrofoam ball to the end. Decorate with sequins, jewels, and/or glitter.

- *Castle Creations.* You can make a castle using a big moving or storage box (cut out windows and a drawbridge if you like), or you can drape a sheet over a table and make a special castle lined with pillows. You may even want to allow the kids to keep the castle up all week. They can act out stories or simply play in their castle.

- *Fairy Tales.* Read or watch stories that include princes or princesses.

- *Royalty in the Bible.* Read about King David (2 Samuel 5:1–5) or the story of Solomon as he was visited by the queen of Sheba (1 Kings 10).

Amazing Animals

Celebrate the uniqueness of God's creation as you enjoy a theme centered on the animal kingdom. You may want to break this down to focus on a different type of animal each day (jungle animals, farm animals, domestic animals), or you could just focus on animals as a whole.

- *Bunny Day.* You may decide to declare a day (when you need some peace and quiet) as bunny day. The kids dress up as bunnies all day. The good news is that bunnies are very quiet creatures, and you may want to allow them to hop along with this theme as you go to the grocery store and run your errands. Just a thought!

- *Animal Dress-Up.* Create your favorite animal's ears using felt and attaching it to a plastic headband. Make a nose and whiskers using a makeup pencil or face paints. You can also buy fake animal noses at party stores. You

may want to use felt or long stuffed socks for tails. Socks
can also be used to cover hands and feet.

- *Animal Entertainment.* Watch movies and television
shows or read books about different kinds of animals.
- *Visit Animals.* Plan a trip to the zoo or a farm to see the
animals firsthand.
- *Animals in the Bible.* Genesis 1:20–25 gives an account
of God's creation of the animals.

Garden Glory

The garden is a wonderful place for both boys and girls. You
can carry out the garden theme indoors or outdoors. If you don't
have a garden, you can create a small one through these simple
ideas.

- *Make tissue-paper flowers.* Use green pipe cleaners for
the stems. Cut 4 x 4 inch squares of tissue paper in a
variety of bright colors. Gather the squares in the center
and secure with the pipe cleaner. Fan out the tissue so it
creates a bloom.
- *Visit an arboretum or gardens somewhere near you.* You
could even have a fun adventure at a local nursery.
- *Decorate clay pots.* You can use stickers or paint or
markers, depending on your kids' ages. You can even do
thumbprints or handprints, depending on the size of pot.
- *Plant seeds or flowers.* If you have a garden, you may
want to plant some seeds or flowers outside on a nice
day. Wear grungy clothes and expect to get a little dirty;
it's OK! You may want to get kid-sized garden tools and
gloves typically available at garden and discount stores.
If you don't have a garden, spread out newspaper and
plant seeds or plants in your newly created planter to set
on the windowsill. Don't forget to water!

- *Create a terrarium.* You will need a large jar (a large pickle jar or gallon jug works best). Lay the jar on its side—you may want to make a foam cradle for it using a Styrofoam block so it doesn't roll. Put dirt in the bottom and gently plant a few seeds, add water, and watch them grow!
- *Read books about flowers and gardens.* I suggest *Planting a Rainbow* by Lois Ehlert (Voyager Books, 1992) or *My Backyard Garden* by Carol Lerner (HarperCollins, 1998).
- *Read in the Bible about plants.* Matthew 13:1–23 tells the parable about the sower and the seeds. In John 15:1–5, Jesus says that he is the vine, we are the branches, and God is the gardener.

Additional themes for preschoolers include alphabet safari (hunting for letters of the alphabet in the world around them), circus celebration, helpers in our community, learning colors, and terrific teddy bears.

The Elementary Years

Outer Space

Count down and blast off to loads of fun for both girls and boys as you explore the wonders of outer space. You may want to load up on aluminum foil and a couple of bottles of silver or white spray paint to carry out this theme.

- *Space Helmets.* Take a plastic gallon jug (clean it out), and cut away the spout and handle to create a simple helmet. You can either spray-paint it or cover it with foil.
- *Power Jet Pack.* Take two two-liter plastic bottles. Spray-paint or cover them with foil. Use silver duct tape to

connect them together. Tie or belt them on your child's back (with spouts down).

- *Space Food.* Tang is always a treat, along with some dried foods in baggies and food bars. Serve on a tray covered with foil.
- *Moon Rock Hunt.* Crumple up aluminum foil, and you have instant moon rocks. You can place little goodies inside and hide the rocks much like an Easter egg hunt.
- *Moon Dust Art.* Purchase a variety of colored sands at a hobby store. Place newspaper over the work area for easy cleanup. Use cardboard as your base, and begin to create a picture. Use Q-tips to spread glue, and then carefully sprinkle the different colors of sand color by color to form a picture. (Use a plastic spoon or curved paper to sprinkle the sand.)
- *Make a rocket ship out of a big moving box.* Paint it white; add the letters *USA* on the side, along with a sticker of the flag. Cut out round windows.
- *Visit a planetarium or science museum.* If there's not one in your area, you could check out one of the several online planetariums on the Internet.
- *Look at the stars through a telescope, or take your sleeping bags outside and gaze at creation.* If you live in a big city, you may need to drive to the outskirts of town to get away from the city lights for better viewing.
- *Read related verses in the Bible.* For example, Psalm 19:1–6 says that the heavens declare the glory of God.

Bug Out

Whether you like bugs or not, your kids will find this theme fun and fascinating. Who knows, you may end up liking the little critters too! You may choose to break this theme down into a different type of bug each day (such as butterflies, spiders, creepy crawlers, jumping bugs, and flying insects).

- *Make a bug catcher.* You will need an empty big plastic mayonnaise jar and a seven-inch square of insect screening or plastic mesh (available at hardware stores). You will also need a wide, heavy-duty rubber band and paints or stickers to decorate the outside of the jar. After decorating the jar, place a stick and some leaves in the jar and go on a bug hunt. Once you find a bug, place the wire mesh over the top and secure with the rubber band. Take a magnifying glass with you on your bug hunt so you can get a good view of the critters.
- *Make bug antennae.* Take a plastic headband and add black pipe cleaners sticking up as antennae.
- *Make a model bug.* Use Styrofoam balls, paint, and pipe cleaners. Add roly-poly eyes (from craft store), and create your own fun and funky insect.
- *Visit a museum of natural history or zoo.* Check in your area for local bug-related exhibits.
- *Read bug books.* My favorites include the Miss Spider series by David Kirk or any of the bug books by Eric Carle, or you can watch *A Bug's Life.*
- Visit www.insects.org or http://teacher.scholastic.com/activities/bugs.
- *Read related verses in the Bible.* For example, Proverbs 6:6–11 teaches us a lesson from hardworking ants.

Around the World in a Week

Fly around the world and get a taste and feel for other cultures and traditions. You may want to keep a map or globe handy to show the kids your destinations. Choose from the following or visit other favorites. I encourage you to visit one country a day so you

119

are able to saturate yourself in the culture. Travel books and magazines will help you to get a better feel for the area you are visiting.

- *Mexico.* Make crepe-paper flowers using large (10 x 10
  inch) squares of colorful crepe paper and thick floral
  wire. Gather a stack of eight squares in the center and
  secure with wire. You can make a bouquet and connect
  the flowers using floral tape. Purchase an inexpensive
  piñata at a party store. Fill it with candy and allow the
  kids to try to hit it with a broomstick to knock out the
  candy. Learn some words in Spanish (visit www.learn
  spanishtoday.com for free online lessons). Prepare tacos,
  enchiladas, or tamales for dinner. Don't forget the tor-
  tilla chips, guacamole, and hot sauce! Decorate the table
  with bright colors and a sombrero, and add to the ambience with Mexican music.
- *France.* Beautiful artwork, incredible cathedrals, and
  magnificent monuments come to mind as you visit this
  European country. Provide an art studio so that the kids
  can create their own works of art. You may want to visit
  an art museum in your area or check out a picture book
  from the library about the Louvre as well as some of the
  other art museums. A search for French cathedrals
  online or at the local bookstore will reveal a wonderful
  tour of some of the most magnificent structures. You
  may want to try to build a model castle or cathedral
  using clay or sugar cubes or small blocks. You may want
  to have the kids create a family crest as a possible art
  project reflecting back to medieval times. Don't forget
  the French bread and cheese.
- *China.* Visit a local Chinese restaurant and see if you
  can purchase chopsticks for the kids (restaurants will
  often give them out free for the advertising). Teach them

how to use the chopsticks and allow them to try to pick up different objects with them. Introduce the kids to a new Chinese dish and egg rolls. Show the kids an example of Chinese writing (you may need the help of the people at the Chinese restaurant again), and see if the kids can duplicate it on a blank piece of paper. Make dancing sticks using the cardboard tubes from coat hangers and taping colorful ribbons to the end. You can also make Chinese lanterns using construction paper. Take an 11 x14 inch piece of paper and fold it in half. Cut slits starting at the folded edge (leave about two inches at the end). Unfold the paper and bring one end to meet the other so it forms a lantern. Staple to secure and add a small handle with more paper. You can hang streamers from the bottom.

- *Africa.* You may want to visit the entire continent or focus on an individual country. Music is an important part of the African culture. I found that www.music uganda.com offers a beautiful selection of African songs that you can listen to online. Of course, the craftsmanship and artistry of the African culture are amazing. Consider a craft of making a wooden beaded necklace or learning the skill of crocheting. The unique animals on the continent of Africa are also a point of interest—zebras, giraffes, lions, hippos, and alligators, to name a few. You may want to check out books or a movie or visit a zoo that has an African animal exhibit.

Additional theme ideas for elementary-age kids include adventures in art, kitchen creations, musical favorites, wonderful weather, and the five senses.

Preteens and Teens

Scavenger Hunt

Scavenger hunts can come in all shapes and sizes. The fun of scavenger hunts at this age is the teamwork, the creativity, and the adventure all wrapped up into one. The most important thing for you to consider is making sure the activity is age-appropriate and works with your kids' personalities. Consider the following ideas:

- *Visual Adventures.* Each team has a camera (could be a disposable or digital camera or a videocamera) and a list of things around the neighborhood they must accomplish (and take a picture of) in order to get points. You can even make them positive things, such as picking up trash, doing a good deed, checking out a library book, walking the dog, or running around a track. The fun is not only in doing the things on the list (and trying to be the first one done) but also in watching the video or viewing the pictures.

- *Nature's Best.* A nature scavenger hunt is always great fun on a nice day. Make a point sheet of things the kids are likely to see on a nature walk (three red leaves, seven acorns, five pinecones, two bugs). Be sure to give each person a bag to put his or her findings in. The person who finds the most on the list wins.

- *Messy Room Competition.* This is not exactly a scavenger hunt, but it works on the point system and can be played by one person or between siblings. As the adult, you will decide how many points the child will get for certain areas of his room. For example, picking up clothes off the floor is worth two points, reorganizing and straightening drawers is worth five, cleaning out the entire closet is ten. You may even hide a bonus point object, which if found counts as another ten points (don't hide it anywhere that they need to make a mess to find it). Set a time limit (say thirty minutes). The person with the most points at the end wins.

Hawaiian Luau

Aloha! You can use this "hang loose" theme for an event, gathering, party, or simply an evening of fun with the family and unique foods and games. Purchase coconuts and pineapples to use as decorations as well as to eat. Plastic leis and flowers are other theme-builder decorations. Fruit kabobs, pork roast, and rice make a great Hawaiian menu. Games include the following:

- *Hawaii Five-O.* Have the kids do some detective work about Hawaii. See if they can find out the famous explorer who found the Hawaiian Islands, the state bird, state motto, state flower, and the most famous king.
- *Fish in the Basket.* Kind of like a carnival game—you provide plastic or stuffed toy fish to toss in a basket. Everyone must stand behind a line. If they get a certain amount in, they win a stuffed animal.
- *Beach Ball Volleyball.* Set up a simple net (could be a badminton net or even a decorative fishing net) and play some beach volleyball, only using a beach ball. You can add more balls into the game if you see the kids can handle it.

Armor of God

Read Ephesians 6:11–17 to prepare for this theme. The apostle Paul tells Christians to be strong in the Lord and in the strength of his might. Then he describes the full armor of God. You can build on this description by making your own armor to help the kids actually see what Paul was talking about. Here are some simple ways to make it:

123

- *Helmet of Salvation.* Use a football helmet or hat, or make a helmet using an empty (and cleaned) gallon milk jug and cutting out the handle and spout. Spray-paint or cover with foil.

- *Belt of Truth.* Create simple belts using poster board strips and tying string or ribbon to the end to fasten. Talk about how belts in the military are used to hang things on and are vital for the survival of a warrior.

- *Breastplate of Righteousness.* Use brown grocery sacks cut down the center with a hole at the top for the head and armholes at the sides. You may choose to spray-paint it silver so it looks like armor.

- *Shield of Faith.* Cut a shield out of a cardboard box. Spray-paint the cardboard silver and add a handle with duct tape. You can put stickers or symbols on the front of the shield.

- *Sword of the Spirit.* Paul calls the sword of the Spirit the Word of God. Talk about how the Bible is sharper than any two-edged sword and how it is vital in fighting the schemes of the enemy (remember Jesus quoted Scripture when he was being tempted).

Additional ideas for preteens and teens include extreme Frisbee, goofy golf, car wash, art-from-trash creations, and decades week.

Family Fun Devotional

Read: Colossians 3:1–2

Talk:

- What are we supposed to focus on in the big picture of life?
- What kind of theme does that give you for your life?
- How can we set our eyes on things above during a typical day?

Do:

Choose one of the theme ideas from this chapter and carry it out with your family.

12

How to Throw a Brilliant Birthday Bash

Ideas are the root of creation.

EARNEST DIMNET

Rejoice with those who rejoice.

ROMANS 12:15

Creative birthday parties make marvelous memories. The parties you plan for your kids will build a lifetime of wonderful reflections. Let me reassure you that even the uncreative sort of person can plan delightful parties. This chapter will equip you with tools so that you can plan a memorable party with ease and not anxiety.

As we learned in the previous chapter, a theme helps turn an ordinary day into an extraordinary one. The same is true with birthday parties. How do you figure out what theme you want to build your party around? Look to your child. What does he or she love? Build a party around it.

Honestly, you can create a party around any theme. Does your daughter love teddy bears? Then a teddy bear picnic party is perfect for her. Does your son want to be a fireman? Then a fireman party or fire truck party or Dalmatian party will be great for him. When kids are young, you should choose the theme for them, but as they get older, you can give them several choices and let them pick their favorite. "Honey, I know you love baseball, trucks, and also rocket ships. Which one do you want to have for the theme for your party?"

Picking your theme is your first step to successful party planning. How early should you begin the planning? I like to say it is a good idea to start thinking of the theme about two months in advance. Now hold on there; don't panic! I simply say this because the longer you give yourself to plan a party, the easier it is to find items to fit the theme. Besides, your child has probably already started reminding you six months in advance that his or her birthday is coming up. Once you have chosen your theme, you can be on the lookout as you walk through stores for things that would work for your party.

Possible Birthday Party Themes

Preschool	*Elementary*	*Older*
Circus	Pirates	Slumber Party
Farm	Airplanes	Sports
Angels	Tea Party	Pizza Party
Bubbles	Bride Party	Super Stars
Animals	Olympics	Scavenger Hunt
Water/Fish	Glad Scientist	Music
Teddy Bears	Western/Cowboys	Art
Dolls	Flowers/Garden	Movie Critics
Trucks	Trains	Fifties
Prince/Princess	Medieval	Spy/007

Party Invitations

How many kids should you invite? That depends on several factors. First, what is the age of the child? The younger the child, the smaller the party needs to be, because younger ones need more nurturing and care. Generally, parents stay at the parties for kids under four years of age. By the time the kids have reached five, they should be able to stay on their own (in fact, they will most likely act better when their parents are not around). Keep the numbers small and easy to manage when the kids are small (say five to eight guests), and then you can increase the numbers as they get older (say eight to twenty guests).

Another factor to think about is whether your guests are going to be boys or girls or a mixture of both. At preschool parties, you typically have boys and girls. Often family friends and their kids are on the guest list. Your own family members and kids typically come as well. As kids get older and enter school, generally the guest list changes to your kids' friends. You may even choose to have a separate party for family and cousins. In these elementary years, your child may want to have a specifically themed party just for boys or just for girls. If you are having an all-boy party, you may want to limit the number to a manageable amount. Generally speaking, it is important to note that girls sit nicely and play at a party, while boys typically run around with lots of energy.

The last factor to consider is your own sanity level. I was a former schoolteacher and could handle twenty-five kids at one time without too much trouble. My sister, who was an accountant, knows her limitations and keeps the numbers low and manageable. You know yourself and your comfort level. Don't compare with what others do; choose what is best for your ability.

Your invitations can fit your theme and with the help of computers can be homemade. Many craft and hobby stores have a variety of fun theme papers, so check out the possibilities at those stores. You can also make your own. Consider a little paper sack puppet for an invitation to a dog party or zoo party or teddy bear party. What about an old 45 rpm record for a fifties party, or a small map for an international party, or a short DVD for a secret spy party?

Your invitation will build your theme before the party even starts. I believe that the cuteness of the invitation is in direct proportion to how many people come to the party! Your invitation builds the excitement, so think outside the envelope. (You can always buy a bigger size at an office supply store.)

Party Activities

You sent out the invitations, and everyone is coming (because the invitations were so cute, of course). Now you need to figure out what you are going to do with these precious little angels as they arrive. Two things I want to tell you from my teacher experience: plan more than enough activities, and make sure they are age-appropriate. I say more than enough activities because often a game that you think will take ten minutes only takes two minutes, and then you have bored kids on your hands and chaos erupts. Better to plan too many activities and throw some out if you don't have time for them, instead of standing there thinking, *Now what do I do with these kids?*

You want to begin with a good arrival activity that the kids can just join into, since nobody arrives at exactly the same time. For younger kids, it may be playing dress-up for a prince and princess party or decorating a hat with stickers for a circus party. For older kids, it may be a simple craft or a creative name tag. An interesting arrival activity allows kids to join in as soon as they walk in the door and makes them feel at home, instead of wandering around with nothing to do. Free play with toys in the back-yard makes a simple yet planned arrival activity as well.

After the kids arrive, then you want to begin the party with a few fun theme-related, age-appropriate games and activities. This may come as a shocker, but younger kids don't like to be blind-folded (so skip pin the tail on the donkey for preschoolers), and they don't seem to understand competition where one person wins a prize. If you want crying on your hands, give one prize to a preschooler. Then you will have three others crying because they didn't get it. We don't want crying. We want smiles, so let's consider what you can do.

Preschoolers love to pretend and to play dress-up, so consider providing a dress-up barrel or making them up to be animals or clowns or astronauts. Playhouses are a hit, and you can fit one to your theme by painting an old refrigerator box (available at appliance stores or moving companies). Consider a castle for a royal theme, a fire truck for a fireman theme, a house for a tea party theme. Simple circle games and songs work well with preschoolers. If parents are at the party, have them join in the circle time with their child sitting in their lap. Reading a short picture book can also be a good activity, mimicking story hour at the library.

Elementary-age kids are activity driven, whether it is doing a craft or a game or a follow-the-leader type of activity. You can provide a theme-related craft such as stringing beads for a dress-up party, making stick horses for a cowboy party, doing simple science experiments for a glad scientist party, or giving ballerina lessons for a ballet party. Supervision is key, so you may want to hire a teenager or an older cousin to help you with the party.

Older kids like to hang out with a little more freedom. You don't need to schedule the party so that every minute is accounted for. Often arrival activities aren't necessary for the older ones, just food and music, so they can sit around and talk until everyone arrives. You only need to plan one or two big activities, such as a football game and a hayride or a crazy soccer game with several different types of games. Perhaps you are planning a trip to get a manicure for the girls and then lunch. Easy and fun. Not too much, not too little.

If you are at a loss for games and activities, thumb through the pages in chapters 14 and 15 for great ideas. Chapter 16 is devoted entirely to slumber parties, which may help you in the planning of an overnight event.

Quick hint! I have found it is helpful to write out the schedule for the party on a poster board and put it somewhere in the party room. Then I can glance at it easily to see what comes next, and my helpers or parents can see what is happening next as well and join in to help. It also helps to have the schedule posted for older kids so they can see when it is time to open presents or eat cake, and you won't have to answer that question over and over again. Just point to the board! The schedule may look something like this:

11:00–11:10	Arrival activity
11:10–11:40	Games and activities
11:40–12:00	Lunch
12:00–12:10	Cake and ice cream
12:10–12:30	Present-opening game, party favors

How long should the party be? For younger kids, I would keep it at one and a half hours. After that amount of time, the people, the sugar, and the activities tend to overload their senses, and they can become a little restless or cranky. For elementary-age kids who are used to the activity of being in school all day, a two-hour party is a nice length. Older kids may want to hang out a little longer. It depends on the activities and how well they know each other. Better to end a party while everyone is happy than to allow it to drag on too long.

Fun Theme Food and Decorations

You can enhance your party fun by making your food fit the theme as well. Now, I want to assure you that you don't have to feed your guests a meal unless the party is during a meal hour. Cake and ice cream are perfect, but even those can have a fun flair. For instance, for a camping party, make a dirt cake (dark chocolate cake and frosting, covered with chocolate cookie crumbs and gummy worms and candy bugs). For a farm party, you can make a pig cake (a simple round cake with pink icing and an iced cupcake for the pig's snout). Actually, you can use the cupcake for a snout on a bear cake or dog cake as well.

If you plan to feed the kids a meal, consider the ways you can serve it to keep the theme going. For an airplane party, serve food on trays as they sit in rows as passengers. One time when I was having a Dalmatian party for my daughter, I fed the kids dog food while they sat on the floor with their dog bowls. Well, not exactly dog food. It was actually trail mix that I put in a box, which I labeled Dog Food. I also gave them sandwiches cut in the shape of dog biscuits. The little doggies loved it! For dessert, we had Dalmatian Delight ice cream. It was really chocolate-chip ice cream, but a name is everything!

Don't forget to feed the parents. If you have parents who have stayed for the party, then you will need to have a table with adult food so they won't stand there drooling. I'm guessing they probably don't want dog food or astronaut food, so provide club sandwiches, chips, and iced tea.

Decorations are not as important as the activities you do at your party. Kids are activity driven. Rarely do you see a child walk into a party and say, "Wow, what great decorations. You must have spent hours!" Pour more of your time and talent into the activities and games. Decorations can help enhance your theme. For instance, if you are having an angel party, you could put white bedsheets all over the floor and cover the tables with cotton to give a heavenly feeling.

The front door is the most important place for your decorations, because this is what most kids will notice. So for a Native American party, kids could crawl through a teepee to get inside. For a dog party, kids could crawl through a large box painted like a doghouse. For a medieval party, make a drawbridge entrance using a box. For a Hawaiian theme, consider paper palm trees. Greet at the door with a black long-haired wig and hula skirt or Hawaiian shirt and hand out leis.

Present Opening

Some party planners recommend skipping the opening of presents at parties because it can be too chaotic. It doesn't have to be chaotic, and I think it is important for the kids to open the presents for the sake of the kids who brought them. Here's how to make present opening part of the activities. Gather the kids around so that everyone can see the birthday child. For preschoolers, it helps to give them a place to sit (a pillow of royalty, a blanket for a dog bed, a cardboard star for circus clowns, etc.).

Two things to remember. First, attention spans are short, so keep the game moving fast and be sure the presents are opened quickly. Second, once a present is opened, your child should say thank you, and then you should put the gift out of sight (I suggest a big box or bag behind the birthday child). It helps to have the birthday child sitting up higher on a chair while the guests are on the floor, so everyone can see.

Gift opening games can include the following:

Musical Gifts. Pass the gifts around the circle as the music plays. When the music stops, the birthday child opens the one he is holding.

Special Presentation. Allow each child to hold the gift he or she brought and then one by one call out their names for a special presentation. For a royal party, you may want to blow a trumpet (a paper-towel tube spray-painted gold) to announce the visiting royalty as they present their gifts. You may want to use a microphone (a toilet-paper tube covered in foil) to announce each celebrity at your Hollywood party as they walk down the red carpet to present their gift. Astronauts could receive patches, firemen receive medals—you get the idea.

Name Draw. Write the name of each child on a card or strip of paper, and put the names into a basket or jar. Draw names one by one. As the winner presents his gift, he receives a little favor or gets a chance to pull a small prize out of a bag. This keeps the interest and anticipation alive.

Statues. Play music as everyone moves around (or dances). When the music stops, the person who is the stillest like a statue gets to present his or her gift. It's always a bit of a judgment call but lots of fun, and eventually everyone gets a turn to present his or her gift.

As you play these games, have an extra gift or two set aside for those kids who may have forgotten their gift or siblings who brought one gift between the two. You want to make sure everyone can participate. You may also want to consider an alternative to people bringing gifts if you feel your child has way too much already. Encouraging everyone to bring a canned good or a toy for a local children's hospital can be a meaningful way of blessing others.

Party Favors

What do you do about party favors? I think we may need to relax a little on party favors. I've been embarrassed bringing my kids home from a party where we brought a nice little gift to the birthday girl but walked away with more in party favors than we spent on the gift. We also want to stay away from a bunch of little plastic trinkets just to fill up a favor bag. Favors should be a memory from the party, and they don't have to be expensive to be meaningful.

In fact, I like for the party favors to come from the things we did at the party, thereby making my party dollar go further. Here are a few examples:

Giddyup, Cowboy. For a cowboy party, we gave out bandannas and sheriff badges as the kids arrived. You can also find inexpensive kids' cowboy hats if it is in the budget. One of the activities we did was go on a trail ride with our homemade stick horses (made with a yardstick and craft-foam head, yarn for the mane). We played some ranch-hand games, such as roping a plastic horse, tossing pennies in a jar, and milking a cow (using a poster with a picture of a cow and white latex gloves filled with milk for udders). After the cookout, we sang by the fake campfire (rolled-up newspapers covered with brown paper for logs and colored cellophane for fire). As the young buccaneers left the party, we handed them a burlap pouch with gold coin chocolate candies inside.

Back to the Prairie. Another example of themed party favors is the Little House on the Prairie birthday party. We did this party for one of my daughters who loved the *Little House on the Prairie* books and television show. As the kids arrived, they decorated drawstring canvas bags. These became their favor bags, and they carried them with them throughout the party. We played school, and the kids got to keep their little chalk slates (found on sale) and chalk. Another activity we did at the party was to make rag dolls out of men's handkerchiefs, and again the dolls went into their bags of goodies. At the end of the party, we gave out some little candy and a big red apple. The party was simple and inexpensive, and the favors were from the activities. At the end of the party, one girl shouted, "This was the best party I have ever been to!" It was actually a simplistic party, back to the prairie days with sack races and wheelbarrow races. Why was it the best? Because it was unique and centered around my daughter's interest. It was a memory in the making!

Designer Originals. My friend Leslie Clayton shares her fantastic idea: "Last year for Claire's tenth birthday, we invited about seven girls to play fashion designer. I had accumulated about eight jean jackets over a year or two (paying as little as five dollars in some cases and then shopping resale stores), and they each got a jacket that they were able to personally design. My always-ready-to-help mom and I set up the dining room like a workshop. I had all kinds of beads, fringe, trim, etc., and then I painted the back of each jacket (using stencils) with the design they wanted. With both of us working, we were able to send the girls home with their jackets the next morning. By planning ahead and buying the jackets on sale and using coupons for the trim at craft stores, I probably spent not much more than I would have for party favors."

Parties in a Nutshell

Hopefully you have gleaned some creative theme ideas as you have read about the party principles in this chapter. As you plan for a birthday party or any kind of special event, remember to pray as you plan. Ask the Lord to lead you and give you new and creative thoughts. Keep your eyes open as you walk through stores and build your theme. Talk about the theme with some of your friends, and see if they have any input as well.

Remember that the most successful parties come down to your attitude and flexibility. Sure, there will be a little glitch here and there. Roll with it. Enjoy your guests and receive them with open arms. Ultimately, it is not the perfect decorations or extravagant games or food that people will remember. Your guests will remember a fun theme offered by a warm and gracious hostess.

Family Fun Devotional

Read: Psalm 139:14–18

Talk:

- Why do we celebrate birthdays?
- From this psalm, what do you learn about the way you were made?
- Go around the table and tell one thing you are thankful for in each family member.

Do:

Which child has the next birthday coming up in your family? Help the birthday person choose a theme centered on something he or she loves or enjoys. Put your heads together to begin planning the event. You will see how much fun planning can be once you get rolling.

Use the following worksheet for all of your party plans.

Party for _____

Theme:

Invitations:

Activities:

Decorations:

Food:

Favors:

13

Every Occasion Can Be a Great Occasion

Creativity involves taking what you have, where you are, and getting the most out of it.

CARL MAYS

Teach us to make the most of our time, so that we may grow in wisdom.

PSALM 90:12 NLT

There are several phrases my dad used to say that ring in my ears to this day. Here are a few:

"Do it now. Don't wait until you get around to it." He actually had a little wooden coin with the word *Tuit* printed on it that he would give to associates. Yes, it was "a round tuit"! On the flip side it said, "Do it now," encouraging fellow businessmen to quit procrastinating and get the job done rather than waiting until they got around to it (or "a round tuit").

"Make a decision and then make it a right decision." Another great phrase, helping us when we didn't seem to have a clear direction in a decision. Dad would say, "Once you have prayed and gathered all the facts, then make a wise decision. Once you have

made a decision, don't look back but move forward through the challenges and make it work."

"Make every occasion a great occasion." This was a reminder to make each meeting, event, and occasion a positive experience.

Although these simple phrases were intended mainly for businessmen or-women, they helped me to be disciplined and focused. They motivated me to move in a positive direction in my personal life. The third quote can be applied in many different ways, but I think it is wisely used on the home front. A fun home celebrates even the simple things. As we celebrate and enjoy each occasion, we build a sense of thankfulness and gratitude for the way the Lord is working in our lives. In this chapter, I want to inspire you to make the most of each opportunity you have to celebrate your family and what is happening in your lives.

Joy in the Required Stuff

Learning to make the best of the chores and homework that we don't want to do helps us persevere and become more disciplined. Let's take a look at a few "unfun" areas of life and see how we can make the best of them.

Laundry and Cleaning. Get the kids to join in the process as much as possible. Sorting socks can be a contest to find who can find the most matches. Cleaning up toys in the den can become a game of Fill the Basket. Laura Arnold, mother of two, shares what she does with her daughter: "Chelsea helps me with the household chores. It started out when she was about eighteen months to two years. She would help by removing the lint in the dryer. Now she puts away the silverware and helps me dust with the feather duster. We always make a big deal about how helpful it is when she helps out around the house. There are many benefits from including her, such as positive reinforcement, self-esteem, sense of accomplishment, and spending time with Mom."

Dinner. Take a moment to write out dinnertime tasks, one on each index card. Put them in a jar or bowl and have each child pick out one (if you have a wide span of ages, you may need to color-code the cards so they pick one that is an age-appropriate task). Tasks can include but are not limited to setting the table, folding napkins, stirring sauce, chopping veggies (older kids), grating cheese (older kids), saying the blessing, clearing the table, cleaning dishes. The cards can be used over and over again for each dinner.

Homework. Prepare a special homework station complete with stapler, sharpener, extra pens, index cards, pencils, and paper. I like to buy inexpensive, colorful office supplies and organizers so the kids have a fresh and motivating place to work. One year I found purple plastic roller carts on sale, so I just rolled the homework station into the kitchen when it was time to work. Try to have a good, nutritious snack ready for the kids when they come home so they can enjoy it while they get to work. Sit down with them and help as needed when they are young. Offer a small reward when they finish their homework. It may be watching a favorite show, calling a friend, reading a book, or using the computer. If your child has been diligent to work on his homework, you may want to allow him to do his reading homework in a cozy place such as a couch or lounge chair. When I know that my kids' homework level is extremely stressful, I'll rub their backs while they are working or make them their favorite snack.

Summer Reading. Think of several fun and unusual places for the kids to do their reading, such as a large bathtub lined with pillows, a window seat, a closet floor, the master bed, or a comfy chair. Write each of these places down on a card and let them choose. Set a designated R&R (reading and relaxation) hour each day so everyone (even Mom) relaxes and reads. My sister, Karen, offered a summer reading store to her kids. She bought fun things for summer, such as pool toys, colorful plastic tumblers, small toys and games, and of course more books! She also offered movie tickets and rentals and concessions. Her daughters earned play money by reading a certain amount of time, and then each Friday the reading store was open for business. Her daughters loved it. Karen started this when her kids were just finishing first grade, and by fifth grade, they loved reading so much they didn't even need the incentives anymore.

Bath Time. Giving the kids a bath doesn't have to be difficult. It can be a wonderful time for interaction and play as well as getting cleaned up. Always be on the lookout for a toy or waterproof book that you can use during tub time. Foam soap or a bottle of bubbles can make the ordinary bath time a lot more enjoyable. As you are washing the kids' hair, pause while you have them lathered up and create funny hairdos (show them how they look in a hand mirror). Perhaps you want to reserve a few songs or a special sing-along CD that the kids sing while in the tub. Consider songs and stories about water or fountains or splashing. Sink or Float can also be a fun tub game as you test out different household objects to guess what will sink or what will float. Remember safety first; always check water temperature and never leave young kids unsupervised.

Bedtime. Make bedtime a special time to listen to your kids and let them know you love them. Share a word or two of encouragement about things you noticed about them during the day. Pray together. You may even want to tell them a short Bible verse that was meaningful to you during the day or read a devotional. My friend Amy shares, "At bedtime, when the kids were little, we would always end our tucking-in time with repeating the words from the wonderful little book *Love You Forever* [by Robert Munsch] to each other. It goes like this: 'I'll love you forever, I'll like you for always. As long as I'm living, my baby (I would say) and my mommy (they would say) you'll be.' We would add, 'Good night, sleep tight, don't let the bedbugs bite.' Then we would blow kisses to each other and pretend to catch them with our hand on our cheek before I closed their doors. It was a precious time and something we say now and then even to this day."

Sick Child. If you have a sick child home from school, make it an occasion to grow closer and bond together. Bring her soup or crackers on a tray with a flower or a funny picture to cheer her up. Rub her back and tell her stories about when you were young. Read some of her favorite books to her. Listen to her. Play a drawing game where you draw on a sketch pad or wipe-off board following her specific directions. ("Draw a line on the right hand side of the page. Draw squiggly lines across the bottom," etc.) She can't tell you what it is supposed to be until the picture is complete. It's always fun to laugh about the creation, as it never quite looks like what the person envisioned.

Relishing Relationships

Our relationships with each other are top priority, second only to our relationship with the Lord. It's easy in the hustle and bustle of our lives to become complacent about celebrating each other and the blessing of each family member. Here are some ways we can emphasize our appreciation of each other.

Dates with Dad or Mom. Each birthday, my dad took me out for a special dinner date, just him and me. I chose the restaurant. It was a great time to talk, practice manners, and feel special. Moms can take their sons out for a special evening as well. It doesn't have to be expensive; even a picnic will do.

Welcome Home. Whenever my kids went to camp or on a mission trip, I would decorate their room and door with signs to celebrate their return. They were simple, with phrases such as, "We missed you!" "We love you!" "Glad you are home."

Notes and E-mails. Write to your kids often, even when they are young. Write them little notes and put them under their pillows. Send them e-mails to let them know you are praying for them. Put notes on their mirrors with a temporary wipe-off marker. Use wipe-off boards and bulletin boards to convey messages as well as encouragement.

Surprise Visits. When your kids are in elementary school, surprise them with a visit during their school lunch, bringing one of their favorite meals. Look for other opportunities when they would enjoy a little surprise visit from you. If they usually ride the bus, surprise them and pick them up on occasion. As your kids are older, you can make a surprise visit to their work just for a moment to say hello and let them know you are thinking about them.

Quality Playtime. Make sure your husband gets special time with the kids. Perhaps the time after dinner can be declared "Daddy playtime." In my family growing up, we used to roughhouse and jump all over my dad. He'd pick us up and put us on his shoulders (watch out for ceiling fans) or hold our hands and swing us around. He would get on his hands and knees and allow us to climb all over him. We loved it!

Celebrating Accomplishments and Special Days

Certainly we want to celebrate the big accomplishments, but don't forget about the small ones, too, such as making a good grade on a test or beating your best time in track practice or finally achieving a forward head roll on the balance beam. You don't have to go overboard, but you can give a gift to your child by sweetly acknowledging some of the little things as well as the biggies. Here are a few ideas:

Special Plate. Purchase a colorful and unique plate at a store or garage sale. You can even write a verse on it or the words *You Are Special* using permanent marker or hobby paint. You may want to make your own at a paint-your-pottery place. The special plate is to be used by the person being honored, whether it is for an accomplishment or a birthday.

Favorite Meal. Celebrate a birthday or an accomplishment with a favorite meal or dessert. Find out from the honoree what he or she would prefer. I've found that tastes change over the years, so keep updated on favorite things.

Cutouts. Use alphabet cookie cutters, or make round cookies and write a letter in the center of each one using icing or small candies. On someone's special day, write out his or her name with cookies. Hand out a different lettered cookie to each family member, and let him or her say an adjective (beginning with that letter) that describes the special honoree.

Fun Flags. Using felt material and felt cutouts and a dowel rod, create a flag for each member of the family. You may want to do this together as a family activity. Each flag should be unique and represent the interests of the individual. Fly the flag to celebrate birthdays, anniversaries, and significant events.

Congratulations Dinner Out. My friend Leslie Wilson shares this idea of celebration: "Each grading period since my children started school, we reward them with a nice dinner out for getting all As on their report cards. Because we typically eat at home, going out is a special treat, and we make the event more meaningful by telling the server the reason for our visit. Occasionally, servers will congratulate the kids or bring them a free dessert. That's even better than getting a freebie on their birthday. During dinner, we discuss their effort and diligence for that nine weeks and raise our glasses in a toast to encourage them to keep up the good work."

Making the Ordinary Extraordinary

There are some days when you have nothing planned, and that's a good thing. It's a blessing for you and your family to relax and not be overscheduled. Relaxation and downtime are vital, but there may be a day when you do want to do a little something extraordinary. Maybe it's a Saturday or a day in the middle of school vacation. At our kids' schools (middle and high school), they are allowed a certain amount of grace days, which must be approved ahead of time by the teachers. We have used a few of those for doing something fun as well. Here are a few ideas to consider:

Movie Day. Rent some of your favorite movies, pop popcorn, and supply candy and soft drinks just like the movie theater. It's fun to take it a step further and give everyone play money to buy movie tickets and concessions. Use a play cash register and set out candy and soda pop on a table for the kids to purchase.

Drama Day. Create a play together. Make up the story or use one that you are already familiar with. Assign parts so that everyone participates. Use the dress-up barrel for costumes. Perform the play for Dad or videotape it to watch and to send to relatives.

Music Day. Listen and learn about different kinds of music. Create your own band by making a variety of instruments from materials that you have around the house. A paper-towel tube and a funnel can become a horn or trumpet. Make drums using coffee or oatmeal cans. Create a xylophone by setting up glasses of water, each with a different amount. Tap the glasses with a spoon for different sounds. Make a stringed instrument using a shoe-box top and putting large rubber bands around it. Play together and make a symphony of sound.

Art Day. Visit an art museum if you have one nearby, or go online and look at a variety of artists. We even had an art bingo set, which helped us put together great works of art with master artists. Encourage the kids to do a little art on their own. You can choose different mediums, such as painting, sketching, papier-mâché, and collages. Allow your kids to discover and explore some of their hidden talents. Consider framing some of their work from art day and lining a hall with the pictures. Invite visitors to see the art exhibition when they come over.

Mystery Trips. My friend Carol Floch celebrates "nothing days" in a creative and unique way. I'll let her tell you about it:

"I love planning surprises and keeping the destination a secret. Sometimes it was a special outing on a day off of school. Sometimes just a fun surprise for a summer day. Usually it was just a day trip, but sometimes a weekend away. Once I even surprised them with a trip to Dallas. (I packed their suitcases all week while they were at school.) They didn't figure it out until we were almost to the airport. Needless to say, they were shocked! The night before or day of a mystery trip, I would tell them what they needed to wear or bring. It helped make traveling part of the adventure, instead of just the destination. It tends to keep everyone in upbeat moods. One time we drove to see friends who had moved to the next state, which was a tremendously fun surprise for the kids! Of course, the kids would hammer me with questions, wanting clues, and they loved to try to guess where we were going, but usually I was pretty tight-lipped! To this day, my kids tend to enjoy car travel and the family time it provides."

Family Meetings

Another wonderful attribute I appreciate about my dad is the fact that he would call family meetings. Often they were on Sunday nights, and they offered a time for us to come together and encourage one another. Our meetings were also an opportunity for us to share with each other what was going on in our lives and offer prayer requests. We would close each meeting by praying for each other.

As we close this chapter, I want to invite you to hear what another one of my dear friends has to say about her family meetings. LaVerne Davis writes:

An exciting and meaningful time for our family is on Sunday evenings at dinnertime. We gather around the dinner table and join hands as my husband [Dana] blesses the food and asks God's blessing upon our family meeting. As we pass around bowls of potatoes, green beans, chicken, and hot dinner rolls, we laugh and share as we prepare to discuss our upcoming week. As mom, I put the family calendar and a pen to take notes at my side.

Our family keeps a big 12 x14 inch monthly calendar posted in the kitchen. The calendar has everything concerning everyone's schedule for the week. All the kids' activities, tests, projects, travel schedule, as well as my speaking engagements, seminars, family church activities, family volunteer activities, etc., are posted.

The meeting starts with Dana telling everyone to think about the upcoming week and inviting everyone to discuss what is on our hearts. Next, I remind everyone what is scheduled on the calendar for every day of the week. As I am sharing, everyone adds anything I may have missed, makes corrections or changes, or asks me to check on something for clarity. After this exciting time of sharing, my husband asks the children if they have anything on their hearts that is troubling or any concerns about school or their activities. He informs the children that Mom and Dad are here to help and they should not be burdened. He tells them we are a family, and we will seek the Lord's wisdom and work together to resolve all concerns.

Then we go around the table one person at a time, sharing any concerns or specific individual comments. When one person is talking, we are to give them our undivided attention, practice skillful listening, and not prejudge or blurt out a solution. As Nick and Megan share, it is amazing the things we learn as parents about each child's life and the way in which each child is different and processes information differently. We take each item shared seriously and discuss it in detail, and when appropriate I make a list of follow-up items. We work to ensure that all items are resolved during the week. As parents, Dana and I do what we tell the children we will do, so that we are always building trust and the children feel that they can come to us with anything at any time.

Dana and I share as well and request prayer for the week. We close the meeting only after everyone has shared and is comfortable concerning the week. Dana opens the meetings with a prayer, and I say the closing prayer. After the meeting is over, I prepare a weekly prayer list for everyone, and I distribute follow-up items as appropriate.

Family meetings are a blessing to our family and have made us a close family and one who trusts one another. The Lord gave Dana this idea, and we give God the glory. When our family meetings are completed, we all have peace! The Lord Jesus has touched us all. Smiles and peace on everyone. It is a miracle! All to His glory.[1]

Family Fun Devotional

Read: Genesis 1:1–5

Talk:

- What do you find amazing about the first day of creation?
- Who is the ultimate authority in taking the ordinary and making it extraordinary?
- When you have trouble thinking of something creative or positive to do, who can you go to for help?

Do:

Make celebration flags for each member of the family. You will need craft glue and fun things to decorate the flags. Visit Wal-Mart or a craft, hobby, or fabric store for supplies. Allow everyone to decorate their own flag with their name and something about themselves on it, although you may need to help younger ones. Staple or glue each flag to a dowel rod. Use the flags to celebrate accomplishments, achievements, birthdays, or significant events. You can fly a flag on a post outside your front door or in your kitchen. You may want to make or purchase a stand to hold the flag when you are displaying it.

step
four

Welcome Friends and Family

When there is room in the heart, there is room in the house.

Danish Proverb

When God's children are in need, be the one to help them out. And get into the habit of inviting guests home for dinner or, if they need lodging, for the night.

Romans 12:13 NLT

We open up the door to fun when we open up our door to others. Enjoy the fellowship of friends and family by creating an inviting atmosphere filled with joy and laughter.

14

Outdoor Games and Adventures

Nature, like a kind and smiling mother, lends herself to our dreams and cherishes our fancies.

VICTOR HUGO

Sing to the LORD with thanksgiving;
make music to our God on the harp.
He covers the sky with clouds;
he supplies the earth with rain
and makes grass grow on the hills.

PSALM 147:7–8

God has provided a wonderful playroom filled with beauty, adventures, and discoveries for kids of all ages. As we step outside, we step into a wonderful world of possibilities. I want to help you take full advantage of the great outdoors through creative games and activities. We all have different outdoor opportunities available to us. Some of you may have a fenced-in backyard, while others live in the city, while others live with wide-open space for miles (and the rest of us are jealous of you). You may even have a park somewhere in the vicinity that is only a short walk or drive away.

Consider the outdoor opportunities that are available to you, and apply the games and activities in this chapter to your situation. Many of the ideas you will find here will work well when you have a number of kids on your hands, so if the neighborhood kids show up at your house or if the cousins come over for a visit, you will have creative fun on hand. Most important, we can rejoice in God's wonderful creation and thank him for providing the perfect playground.

Outdoor Games

Terrific Tag Games

The thrill of the chase and the excitement and strategy of outrunning the person who is "it" make tag games a hit for kids of all ages. In a typical tag game, one person is designated as "it" and chases the others, trying to tag them. If a player is tagged, he or she becomes the new "it." You can also play elimination tag, in which the tagged person is out of the game. The last person left without being tagged becomes the new "it." You can choose "it" by drawing names out of a hat or by choosing a number between one and thirty. The closest one is "it." You can also draw straws (the short one is "it") or pick candies (the one who gets the red one is "it"). Here are some variations of the typical tag game:

Shadow Tag. Instead of tapping the runners, the person who is "it" simply steps in the person's shadow. For the best shadows, play in the late afternoon.

Freeze Tag. Tagged people stand like frozen statues when they are tagged. Other runners can tag them and unfreeze them.

Chain Tag. Best with a large group, the first person tagged joins hands with "it," and they both begin to chase others. Each person tagged joins the chain. Only the two players on the outside of the chain can tag. Keep going until everyone is a part of the chain. The last one is the new "it."

Airplane Tag. Everyone on the ground is fair game to be tagged by "it." The players are safe if they are aboveground (sitting on a swing, stepping on the ladder of a slide, or standing on steps).

Hat Tag. You will need an old hat for this one. The person who is "it" must tag the person wearing the hat. The person being chased may toss the hat to another person if "it" gets too close. If the person with the hat is tagged, then he or she becomes the new "it."

Fun and Easy Ball Games

If you have kids in your home, it is a good idea to have a supply of balls as well. Here are a variety of games to consider:

Circle Ball. Circle up (or if you have enough kids, create two circles) and pass the ball around the circle. Start with tossing it to the player on the right. Once the ball has gone around once, you can vary the way you pass it: bounce it once, or pass between the legs or behind the back. If you have two circles, they can compete to see who gets the ball around the circle the fastest. (Ages 3–8.)

Soccer Circle Ball. Circle up again, only this time the ball is on the ground and players kick it back and forth, keeping it within the circle. The game can be light and simple for young ones, but it can be challenging for older kids as the pace picks up. (Ages 4–10.)

Racketless Tennis. You will need a tennis ball and some chalk for this game. No net is needed, just a flat surface on a driveway, playground, or wide sidewalk. Use the chalk to draw a rectangle about twelve feet long and six feet wide. Draw a line down the middle, which serves as the net. The first person serves the ball by bouncing it once and hitting it with the palm of his hand. The ball must land in the opponent's court. The ball is volleyed back and forth until one of the players misses the ball, doesn't get it across the line, or hits it out of bounds. Players only score when they are the servers. Play to eleven points, but the winner must win by two points, so if the score is 10–11, play continues until someone has a two-point lead. (Ages 7–15.)

Races and Relays

Your most important job in hosting a race is determining the course. Where are the start and finish lines, and is it a clear and safe path? Choose teams randomly (don't ever have kids or captains pick their teams, as feelings always get hurt). I believe it works best to draw colors (colored strips of paper or material) out of a bag to form teams. You can even divide by hair color, eye color, birthdays, or alphabetically. Then even up the teams before you begin.

Back-to-Back Race. Set up two goalposts or chairs about twenty-five feet from your starting line. You will need about ten feet between the two teams. The players on each team stand back to back, linking elbows and running in this position (sideways). Each couple runs to their goalpost, circles it, and then returns to tag the next couple on their team. The team to finish first is the winning team. (Ages 10–14.)

Bunny Hop Relay. Mark two lines on the ground at least fifteen feet from each other for the start and turnaround lines. Divide kids into two teams, lined up single file behind the starting line. At the command "Go!" the first player on each team hops like a bunny to the turnaround line and continues back to the starting line. After she crosses the finish line, the next player in line goes. The first team with all of its bunnies down and back is the winner. (Ages 3–8.)

Kangaroo Hop Relay. This is a variation of the bunny hop relay for older kids. A little different type of hop is required. This time, the kangaroos stand with both feet together and keep both feet together as they land and add a little more spring to their stride. With this relay, the turnaround line should be about thirty feet from the start. (Ages 8–12.)

Sack Races. You will need either a burlap sack or a pillowcase for each player (or you could make it a relay and provide one for each team). Play only on the grass or a soft surface, such as sand at the beach. There will be loads of laughter and fun as players try to hop across the finish line in their sacks with a few stumbles along the way. Mark the start and finish lines with sticks or ropes, making the course about thirty feet. You may want to run this race several times and watch the kids get better and better. (Ages 7–12.)

Tunnel Ball. Begin by marking start and finish lines about thirty feet apart. This game is best played on a large, flat surface, and you will need one ball for each team. Players for both teams line up single file behind the starting line and spread their legs out. At the command "Go!" the player at the front of each line rolls the ball through the tunnel of legs on his team. Players are free to help the ball stay in the tunnel. As the last person receives the ball, she runs to the front of the line with the ball and sends it down the tunnel again. Slowly, each line will progress forward. The first team to make it entirely across the finish line wins. (Ages 6–12.)

Just Plain Fun Games

Some outdoor games are simple and fun for everyone. You will find that most ages enjoy the following:

The King's Treasure. Draw a large circle with chalk (or you can use shoes to form a circle in the grass). Kids circle up with one person in the center. You will need a bag of coins, a beanbag, or something that is easy to grab to serve as the king's treasure. The king in the middle stands over the treasure to guard it. Everyone in the circle slowly tries to sneak up and grab the treasure without being tagged. They are safe if they are back outside the circle. If they are tagged, they must sit on the outer circle. The first one to get the treasure is the next king. (Ages 5–13.)

Obstacle Course. An obstacle course can be set up in a number of different creative ways in your own yard. You will need to make sure it is age-appropriate and safe. Some of my favorite items to use for an obstacle course are a box, a jump rope, a chair, a ball, and a basket. For starters, consider having the kids crawl through the box, then they must jump three times with the rope, sit on the chair, and toss the ball in the basket. You can make a simple course for young ones and a more difficult and longer course for older kids. Items to add to the obstacle course include a hula hoop, plastic slides, a mini exercise trampoline, sprinklers (if it is hot), and a fabric tunnel. (Ages 3 and up.)

Sheep and Wolf. This is a variation of hide-and-seek, only the hiders and seekers end up changing roles. You will need to choose one person to be the wolf while all the rest are sheep. Determine a central home base (a tree stump, fountain, porch step). Remember, safety is the first rule of business, so make sure you establish boundaries and places that are off-limits. At first the wolf hides while all the sheep close their eyes until the wolf lets out a howl. The sheep all begin to search for the wolf. When a player spots the wolf, he yells, "I see a wolf!" The wolf then chases the sheep, trying to tag them before the sheep reach home base. If a sheep is caught, he or she becomes the next wolf. If everyone makes it to home base safely, then the wolf continues for another round. (Ages 5–12.)

Red Light, Green Light. One person is chosen to be "it" and stands about twenty or thirty feet away from the starting line, with his back turned to the group. The person then shouts, "Green light!" which is the signal for everyone to begin moving forward. When he says, "Red light!" everyone is supposed to freeze in position. The person who is "it" turns around immediately to catch anyone who is still moving. If he sees any movement, he calls those people by name and sends them back to the starting line. The person who is able to tap "it" first without being detected wins and gets to be the next "it." (Ages 5–10.)

Follow the Leader. Choose one leader who will direct the rest of the group with his or her words and example. Walk like a monkey to the mailbox, act like you are swimming across the yard, and hop on one foot to the tree are a few possibilities. As the adult, you may want to be the first leader. Keep the kids' ages and abilities in mind, and remember to maintain safety at all times. (Ages 5 and up.)[1]

Bubbles

Oddly, I have found that kids of any age love bubbles. Yes, even teens enjoy mixing this homemade recipe and searching for unique objects they can use for creating bubbles of all sizes. Young kids love the opportunity to chase and pop the bubbles or have a parade of bubbles. Here's the formula:

5 cups water
¼ cup glycerin (available at pharmacies)
½ cup dishwashing liquid (Joy or Dawn)

Mix together in a large bowl and then divide into smaller containers. (Plastic butter tubs and yogurt containers are perfect.)

For your bubble makers, you can use a paper-towel tube, a plastic strawberry basket, pipe cleaners formed in different shapes, serving spoons with holes, or straws. For bigger bubbles, use large rings or form shapes using a wire coat hanger. For giant bubbles, pour the formula into a baby pool and make bubbles using a hula hoop. You can even stand in the center of the hoop and make the bubble rise around you as you lift the hoop up.

Happy Trails

Hiking and camping can offer a tremendous and fun opportunity for family bonding and friendships. Who can place a value on the togetherness that happens when you are forging a stream or hiking through the woods or climbing a small mountain as a family?

One can never underestimate the conversations that take place sitting around a campfire or sharing a tent together. Even if your family is not the camping type, you can still consider a family hike or walk together. Honestly, our family has only been camping in tents out in the woods once, but we still count it as a great family memory. We have had many walks and hikes together that served as wonderful outdoor experiences for us.

Keys to Happy Camping. There are certain ways to ensure a happy time while camping. The first is to have a flexible attitude. It's essential to have the spirit of "We can do it!" or "Let's make the best of it!" when challenges come our way. Proper planning for food and supplies makes things run much more smoothly. Keep camping at your level of comfort; don't try to be extreme campers, especially your first time. If you are new to camping, it helps to go camping with another family that is more experienced. Always be prepared for rain, no matter what the weather forecast predicts. It is also a good idea to know the hazards of the area so that you put food away and steer clear of everything from bears to bees. Visit gorp.away.com for camping advice and info.

Wonderful Walks. Walks offer wonderful opportunities for exploration, even if you are in your own neighborhood or nearby fields or public parks. Saturdays and Sundays are good, relaxed days to schedule an adventure. Bring the dogs along! Use this as an opportunity to observe, touch, and feel nature. You may have something you want to collect on the journey, such as rocks or leaves or pinecones. (Bring along a bag or shoe box to carry your treasures.) Try to collect a walking stick for each family member. Do a little research ahead of time to be on the lookout for certain birds or plant life, and bring along binoculars or a magnifying glass for further observation. You may want to bring the camera as well.

The Fire Pit. Several years ago, we bought a simple fire pit for the backyard and set some chairs around it. Over the years, the kids' friends as well as our own family have enjoyed hanging out at the pit. Roasting marshmallows is always a great activity. The beauty of a fire pit is there is something warm and inviting about a crackling fire. We have been known to sit for hours and talk. So whether you are at a campsite sitting around an open fire or in your backyard with a fire pit, use these moments to create meaningful conversations. It's also a wonderful atmosphere for sharing family devotionals or using some of the conversation starters from chapter 9.

Nature's Arts

Nature is an open classroom filled with wonder and discoveries waiting to be made. Here are some simple ideas you can do with your kids to make wonderful outdoor memories:

Mud Pies. Bring out some old plastic bowls, plastic containers (whipped cream or butter tubs are perfect), plastic measuring cups, and plastic spoons to make your own mud pies. You may also want to use some baking flour to make it more interesting. Old clothes are a must for this messy but memorable activity. Allow the kids to scoop up mud from a rarely used place in your yard or garden. Mix in flour and water and stir. Pour into tubs and allow to dry in the sun just for fun. The joy is in the measuring, mixing, stirring, and playing in the dirt!

Tree Bark Rubbings. You will need paper and several big crayons with the paper removed. Hold the paper against a tree and rub the paper with the side of the crayon. Look for a variety of trees so that you can get different features with each one. After everyone has had the chance to make several rubbings, bring them together and compare the different types of bark. You may choose to glue a few of them to a big piece of construction paper and make a collage.

Have Sketch Pad, Will Travel. Provide a sketch pad for each child, along with colored pencils or markers. Be sure to bring a blanket along as well. Take a walk outdoors to a place of natural beauty or interest. It may be a garden or a beautiful tree or a little waterfall. Put the blanket down on the ground so everyone can have a place to sit and observe. You may want to call attention to the variety of colors, light, or shadows. Talk about how the colors change throughout the seasons in the leaves and ground and sky. You may want to point out angles and perspective to older kids. Allow the kids to create their masterpieces, and have an art exhibit or show displaying the pictures when you come home.

Natural Art Productions. You will need gallon-sized Ziploc bags, cardboard, and glue for this project. Give each child a Ziploc bag as you take a short walk or excursion outside. Encourage them to gather a variety of items to be used for their art, such as pebbles, sand, leaves, and acorns. You can complete this project at home or on the back porch. Ask the kids to close their eyes and imagine a picture they can create with the items they have gathered. Then, using the glue, have them create the picture on the cardboard.

Outside Relaxation

As we think about all the activities to enjoy outside, let's not overlook the beauty of simply relaxing or resting outdoors. Bring sleeping bags or an old quilt or blanket to a grassy area (free of ants) in your backyard or local park. You may want to choose a place in the shade of a tree if it is a hot day. Enjoy a simple lunch or dinner together (a sandwich, chips, and drink will do).

After lunch (and maybe a little running and playing), tell the kids to lie on their backs and close their eyes. Ask them to be very still and simply use their ears to listen to the sounds of the outdoors. Encourage the kids to relax and enjoy the fresh air and sweet smells and sounds of nature. After a little time of no talking, just listening (hopefully), let the kids tell about the sounds they observed as they rested.

Nature often reminds us that we don't always need to be running and doing. We can enjoy the beauty of creation by slowing down and taking it in through the simplicity of a porch swing or a quilt spread out on the grass. My hope is that we can enjoy not only the outdoor adventures and activities but also the natural refreshment that God's great creation brings to our souls.

Family Fun Devotional

Read: Psalm 19:1–6

Talk:

- What do we learn about God as we observe his handiwork in creation?
- Can you think of something specific in nature that especially turns your thoughts toward God and makes you want to praise him?
- Take a moment to pray and thank God for his marvelous creation that you can enjoy.

Do:

Choose a clear evening when you can go outside and observe the stars together. You may want to drive beyong the reach of the city lights to be able to see the stars better. Check out a book from the library that will help you find the constellations and locate some of the planets. Bring along a telescope if you have one.

15

A Simple Guide to Indoor Fun

The whole world is yours, and you can explore it all again as you play with a child.

GWEN ELLIS

The house of the righteous contains great treasure.

PROVERBS 15:6

Texas summers can be painfully hot, with temperatures above 100 degrees for days on end. Needless to say, the kids and I spend most of those days indoors. Don't get me wrong; I'm not whining about our weather, because the flip side of those hot summers means that we have fairly mild winters. Those of you in the north who shovel five to ten inches of snow have your share of indoor days as well. No matter where you live, even in those continually temperate states, you will face days when you must entertain the kids inside instead of outside.

This chapter is your guide to indoor sunshine on a rainy day. I want to give you a quick and easy reference to simple fun with kids when you are stuck inside those proverbial four walls.

Nothing too elaborate here, just quick and manageable activities so you can create an atmosphere of fun with minimal preparation.

Kitchen Creations

Your kitchen offers a tremendous opportunity to bake, create, and play.

Rice Tub. Lay an old bedsheet down on the floor and place a plastic tub in the center. Fill the tub full of uncooked rice. (I buy large bags from the warehouse stores.) The kids sit on the floor around the tub to play. First allow them to feel and touch the rice, running their hands through it. Then add plastic scoops, measuring cups, spoons, play cars, and other little toys for the kids to enjoy a sort of indoor sandbox. Make sure the kids understand that all rice stays in the tub, although inevitably there will be a few strays. When you are finished, you can shake any stray rice back into the tub. You may want to buy a large tub with a tightly sealed lid so you can bring the rice tub out again and again. I used the rice tub when I needed to write bills. The kids would play with it in close range while I focused on the bills at the kitchen table.

Taffy Pull. This is a great activity that encourages teamwork and togetherness. Use the following recipe for a delightful time:

Molasses Taffy

½ cup butter	1 ½ cups boiling water
2 cups sugar	½ tsp. vanilla extract
1 cup molasses	Plastic wrap

Melt butter in a large pot; add sugar, molasses, and water and boil to soft-ball stage (234–238 degrees). Turn into a buttered shallow pan. As mixture cools around sides, fold toward center. When cool enough to handle, pull until porous and light colored, using tips of fingers and thumbs.

(You may want to give each person disposable plastic gloves.) Add ½ teaspoon vanilla extract. Cut into small pieces with a sharp knife or scissors, and arrange on slightly buttered plates to cool.

Play Dough. Kids can join in the fun of making the dough as well as playing with it. Here's a simple recipe that will keep for weeks in a Ziploc bag in the fridge. Provide a workstation for each child, and help your kids measure and stir their own dough. I suggest laying waxed paper down at each workstation for easier cleanup when you are finished making the dough. You will need:

Food coloring, various colors
¼ cup water
1½ cups flour
½ cup salt
¼ cup vegetable oil

Before you begin, allow each child to choose the color of dough he wants to create, and add several drops of food coloring to the water accordingly. It's fun to watch the color disperse in the water before stirring it up.

In a large bowl, mix the dry ingredients together, then slowly stir in the water and oil until the dough reaches a good consistency. The kids can take the dough out of the bowl and knead it with their hands. Encourage the kids to make figures out of the dough or build a structure. You can also roll it out and use cookie cutters to create shapes.

Veggie Stamps. You will need construction paper, paint, small paper plates or bowls, and vegetables (zucchini, peppers, onions, carrots, etc.). As the adult, you should be the one to cut the veggies in half. Dip the cut half into the paint (slough off excess) and press onto paper. Notice the unique patterns that are made by the different objects. You can vary this activity by cutting a potato and carving it into a shape to use as a stamp. Choose another day to make fruit stamps. Apples make especially interesting stamps.

Pasta Games and Art. Uncooked pasta can offer a play-filled afternoon. Purchase a variety of shapes and sizes of pasta. Pour them into a tub and play with them much like the rice tub. Place several jars or plastic tubs in front of each child, set the timer, and see how many they can separate by shape into their jars before the timer runs out. To bring out your artistic talents, decorate juice and soup cans with noodles. Dip the pasta pieces in craft glue and then place them on the can. Spray-paint the can when you are done and you have a delightful new pencil holder.

Plastic Play Drawer. For busy toddlers and preschoolers, it is helpful to designate one low drawer in the kitchen as the play drawer. Fill the drawer with plastic measuring cups and spoons of all sizes, as well as plastic bowls and cups. Make it clear that they can pull out this particular drawer and enjoy its contents. When the kids are finished, show them how to put all items back in the drawer, then encourage them to do the cleanup themselves as they can. Help them understand that all other drawers are off-limits, or you may want to safety-proof all of them except that one. As kids get older, the drawer can be used for school supplies or a place to keep small gifts and rewards.

Unwinding the Imagination

Through crazy crafts and wonderful art, you can use your imagination to create some amazing indoor creations.

Silly Sock Puppets. Plan a puppet show and create the puppets. First help the kids think of or choose a story to portray or a simple show to perform. It may be one they are familiar with, or they may want to create their own story. You could also have them create the members of a singing group to lip-sync a song from a CD.

Spend a little time writing the script and deciding what characters you need. Now create those characters using socks. Go to the famous sock drawer. (You know, the one that is filled with socks that have no matches.) Use yarn for hair and craft eyes, pompoms, or markers for the eyes and nose. (The nose should be the big toe part of the sock.) The wilder, wackier, and crazier the better. You may want to videotape the production for posterity or simply to have a great laugh.

Budding Authors. Give the kids the opportunity to express themselves through pictures and story by creating their own children's book. You will need plenty of plain white paper and some heavy cardboard or colored cardstock. Tell the kids you want them to create a story. Encourage them to sketch out what they are thinking or write out their thoughts before they actually begin the pages of the book. This project may take several days to complete, depending on how seriously they take it. Younger kids can draw the pictures, and you can write the words for them underneath. Allow the creativity to flow. When their book is complete, take it to an office supply store and have it spiral-bound. You may want to consider laminating the cover. Some printers have book-binding capabilities, so check out what is available in your area. You may even want to make copies to send to grandparents.

Designer Hats. Begin with an inexpensive straw hat or baseball cap, and make it into a hat extraordinaire. Visit a fabric or craft store for supplies such as feathers, sequins, jewels, appliqués, patches, buttons, and fabric remnants. Glue, staple, and/or tape the additions to your hat. See who can create the most outrageous or silly hat, and don't forget to take pictures. You may choose to make your own hats from folded newspapers.

Special Scrapbook. Never underestimate the joy of scrapbooking together. Boys or girls, young or old—all can participate and enjoy working together. Sort through boxes of old photos together, laughing and crying along the way! You may want to make a trip to a craft store to purchase scrapbook materials or make your own. You will want to add stickers, quotes, and little thoughts along the way. Some memory trinkets can fit into the book as well, such as a certificate, birthday card, or award patch. As you work on the big family version, allow younger ones to work on a simple or play version, using stickers, markers, and kid scissors. One day when my kids were about ten and eleven, I told them to gather their favorite pictures, and I took them to a scrapbook place where they each picked out their own album and stickers. We worked for hours together, and they continued to keep up their scrapbooks on their own. I count it as one of my favorite mother-daughter days.

Puzzles. Kids feel a sense of accomplishment when they finish putting a puzzle together, but they will feel an even greater sense of accomplishment when they take part in making the puzzle. You can either have the kids draw a colorful picture on a large, thick piece of construction paper or search for a beautiful full-page picture from a magazine and glue it to paper or cardstock. Allow each child to make his or her own puzzle. Use clear contact paper to strengthen the puzzle, then cut the picture into puzzle pieces. Older kids can cut their own. You may want to determine how easy or difficult you want the puzzle to be (depending on your kids' ages) before you start cutting. Place each puzzle in a separate large envelope or Ziploc bag with the creator's name on it. It's fun to play a game such as Pass the Puzzle. Everyone sits at the table with one puzzle in front of them. When the bell rings, everyone begins to put their puzzle together, but every fifteen seconds the bell is rung and the players shift one seat to the right to work on the next puzzle. The players continue to shift every fifteen seconds until all puzzles are finally complete. Lots of smiles for kids of all ages. Keep the puzzles to bring along on trips or for waiting rooms.

Games in the Great Indoors

There are lots of entertaining games for kids that you can play indoors with just a little creativity! Here are a few:

Lie Down and Listen. Clear a large area in a carpeted room. Ask the kids to lie down on their backs. You may want to give them bath towels to lie onto help them identify their own space. As they lie there, tell them that this is a time to use their ears, so they need to close their eyes and keep their mouths quiet. Ask them to think about what noises they hear. (They may hear the dryer running or the dog snoring or cars going by.) Allow them to tell you one sound when you call their name. Now create some secret sounds (crinkling paper, thumbing a comb, tapping a pan or jar, blowing up a balloon). After each noise, see if someone can raise his or her hand and guess the sound. You may want to gently place a washcloth over your kids' eyes so they won't peek.

Hot or Cold. Children close their eyes while you hide an object or small surprise somewhere in the room. Begin by giving out one clue or hint. As a child gets closer to the object, say the child's name and that he is getting warmer. If he gets farther from the hidden object, he is colder. The one who finds the object gets to hide it for the next round. You can expand the game to cover other rooms of the house. You can also play other hidden object games, similar to an indoor Easter egg hunt, by hiding small toys or stuffed animals around the house. The person who finds the most wins. A treasure hunt with clues to lead to the treasure also makes for a great game.

Simon Says. One person is designated as Simon while the others follow the instructions. This is a great exercise for strengthening children's attention span and ability to follow instructions. Start off with simple tasks (stand up), but then increase the instructions to several tasks at one time (stand on one foot, hold your nose, stick out your tongue). The instructions must begin with the words "Simon says" in order for them to be followed;

otherwise no one carries out the instructions. The more you play, the better you become as an instructor and as a follower. You can vary this timeless game by giving the instructions in another language. The kids still must listen for the "Simon says," only it may sound like "Simon dice" (see-mon dee-say).

Newspaper Wars. Leslie Wilson tells about one of her family favorites: "My son Reese learned about this activity in preschool. First, the whole family has to make ammunition that consists of newspaper wadded into balls. When you each have several dozen, you lay down the rules and start the 'fight.' My husband has been known to turn one of our tables on its side to use it for a fort. It's a lot of work (thirty minutes to an hour) for a short game (ten minutes of screaming chaos), but my kids beg us to have newspaper fights!" This game works well for ages four to ten.

Indoor Campout

When at least five of my friends told me their favorite indoor idea was to have an indoor campout, I knew there was something special about this idea. I'm warning you right now: this could become an annual event for your family or friends. Choose an evening and declare it camp night. You may want to choose a day when there is no school the next morning. The point is to pretend you are camping out, but in reality you are in your own family room. Bring in the sleeping bags, pitch a tent if you can (bedsheets will do the trick), and start a fire in the fireplace.

Prepare a camp dinner, complete with hot dogs, beans, and chips. You can even make s'mores by heating the marshmallows in the fireplace, or use the oven on low broil just to brown them (watch them closely). S'mores are simply a sandwich made of graham crackers on the outside and a chocolate bar and a large, melted marshmallow on the inside. Other foods to consider are hamburgers, popcorn, trail mix, granola, raisins, and peanuts.

Of course, the campfire is an important focus when camping out, but if you don't have a fireplace, you can create a fake campfire by rolling up newspapers to make logs. You can either spray-paint them brown or cover them with construction paper. Use orange, yellow, and red clear plastic wrap to look like flames. Go the extra mile by adding twinkling Christmas lights (which you can also use for stars in the sky). You can also purchase candles or incense with a woodsy smell. One friend told me her kids set out stuffed animals to serve as the outdoor wildlife, and they played nature or jungle sounds on the CD player to create the outdoor ambience.

Backpacks are another ingredient for camping success. Create simple ones by taking a grocery sack and cutting away the top portion of three sides (five inches from the top), leaving one side intact to serve as the top flap of the backpack. Use the portion you cut off to cut in two and fold to create straps, which you can staple to the backpack. Use Velcro to fasten the flap, and allow your young campers to decorate the outside with markers and stickers. They can use the backpacks as they search for pinecones that you have hidden around the house (like an Easter egg hunt).

Binoculars can be added to the backpack. You can make these by simply taking two empty toilet-paper tubes and covering them with black construction paper. Use a ribbon or yarn for the strap, and you have some happy campers on your hands. If you have a compass, bring it out and show the kids how to use it. Turn the lights out and read, and make shadow figures using your flashlights.

You can go as far as you want with the indoor campout! Untold adventures await you and your family in the wilderness of your own living room. Keep a camp journal so you can record your experience year after year. One thing is for sure: you will make wonderful memories for your happy campers.

Family Fun Devotional

Read: 1 John 4:7–12

Talk:

- When is it most difficult to get along with and show love to brothers and sisters?
- Why do you think it is important to show loving-kindness to family members?
- Where does love come from?

Do:

You guessed it! Plan an indoor family campout. Let everyone in on the action, assigning responsibilities to each family member. At the actual campout, lead a devotional time by flashlight. Read 1 Corinthians 13:1–8, and talk about what love should look like in a family.

16

Survival Tips for Sleepovers and Slumber Parties

To all, to each, a fair good-night,
And pleasing dreams, and slumbers light.

SIR WALTER SCOTT

We also pray that you will be strengthened with his glo-
rious power so that you will have all the patience and
endurance you need.

COLOSSIANS 1:11 NLT

It's going to happen. You can't avoid it. At some point in your kids' growing-up years, they are going to ask if they can have a slumber party or sleepover. You can make excuses for ten years, or you can face your fears. Actually, slumber parties can be a lot of fun for both you and the kids. With good planning and a few creative ideas, you will make it through with a smile on your face.

What are you going to do with a bunch of kids for fourteen hours or more? Allow me to walk you through a plan that can work whether you are hosting a few kids for a sleepover or a team of kids for a slumber party. Pick, choose, and glean ideas from this plan to fit the type of situation that you have at the time. Personally, I do not suggest sleepover parties for kids less than nine years of age, since some still get homesick. Carefully consider the age and how many kids you can handle and still keep your sanity.

Mean, grouchy parents can put a damper on a fun event. I went to a slew of slumber parties in my younger days, and the stellar ones that stand out in my mind are the ones where the hosts were inviting and were glad that we were there (or at least they acted that way). A few disaster slumber parties remain in my memory where the parents griped and complained the whole night. Granted, we weren't the quietest kids on the block, but we weren't wild banshees either.

There is a happy middle ground for the slumber party hostess between setting parameters and preparing yourself. Yes, the hostess should have certain expectations about noise, lights-out, and general house rules. But the hostess should also recognize that this is not going to be a nice and quiet typical evening at home. You may need to take a nap to prepare for the event, because your state of mind and your attitude will make a difference in the tone of the party. I also want to encourage you to pray about all the activities of the evening, asking the Lord to bless them and keep everyone safe. As you pray, you will find a sense of calm as you cast your cares into God's hands and seek him for direction.

Slumber Schedule

You will find it very helpful to have a schedule for the evening—not a rigid plan that you must stick to but a frame of reference to keep the kids busy in a positive direction. If left with nothing to do, kids tend to get silly and sometimes out of control. The point is they simply want something to do, and you can give them things to do without micromanaging every minute.

Here's a good general schedule for a sleepover. You may want to rearrange a few things to fit your plans, but this will give you an idea of a smart strategy for the evening's events.

6:30 p.m.	Arrival activity
7:00 p.m.	Dinner and dessert
8:00 p.m.	Tiring activities
10:00 p.m.	Refreshments
11:00 p.m.	Change into pajamas
11:30 p.m.	Movie/lights-out
8:30 a.m.	Breakfast
9:00 a.m.	Morning activity
10:00 a.m.	Out the door

We'll examine each of these individually, but before we do, I want to give you just a few important points. First, as much as possible, do not provide caffeinated drinks or an overabundance of sugary foods. We want our precious angels to go to sleep at some point in the evening, so we should do everything we can to encourage that to happen. Also during those middle school years, there can be a desire for kids to sneak out. You need to guard against this and prevent it, since it is unsafe and other parents have entrusted you with the care of their kids. Make sure your own child knows this type of action will not be tolerated and there will be severe consequences, which include calling the guests' parents. That usually stops them right there.

Evening Events

Let's break that schedule down into bite-size pieces so that you have some good, hearty ideas to chew on as you plan.

Arrival Activity. Start the evening with something the kids can jump into as they arrive. For boys, it may be tossing a football, shooting hoops, or playing pool or foosball. For the girls, consider a craft such as decorating nightshirts or pillowcases with permanent markers or paint pens. Be sure to put cardboard inside the shirt or pillowcase so the paint won't stick the two sides together. You may also want to provide large plastic cups for the kids to use throughout the party. They can decorate their own cup with stickers, markers, and paint. All of these items can become part of the kids' party favors as well. If this is a birthday celebration, provide a big poster on which everyone can write a special greeting to the birthday child as they arrive.

Dinner. You may want to start off with a creative cooking activity in which guests participate in preparing the meal. Divide the kids into small groups or couples, and give each group a workstation in the kitchen, complete with recipe and items they need to put the recipe together. The kids feel a sense of satisfaction that they had a part in the preparation. An apron would make a fun party favor for your chefs. Allow everyone at the party to sign it with permanent markers. Making and decorating pizzas would be another fun way to prepare dinner, rolling out the dough and decorating with a variety of toppings. Even guys enjoy this activity, as they have fun working with the dough. If creative cooking isn't your bag, hamburgers and hot dogs on the grill make a perfect dinner as well.

Dessert. It is wise to offer dessert early in the evening so that the effects of the sugar are worn off as the kids play and participate in activities. If it is a birthday, you can provide cake and ice cream. Consider other dessert ideas, such as making your own ice cream sundae, decorating cookies, or creating the world's biggest banana split. One year for my daughter's birthday, I divided the kids into teams and gave each team a giant cookie. The teams were given icing and sprinkles and were instructed to make a Happy Birthday cookie for my daughter. It was fun and amazing to see what the girls could do with one simple cookie. For a party in the heat of summer, snow cones could make a great dessert as well.

Surprise Bags. The element of surprise can keep things interesting for your guests. You can choose to give out surprises throughout the evening and make it similar to a door prize give-away. Everyone's name is in the hat, and every hour at the top of the hour you have a drawing for a fun prize. They can be simple prizes, such as lip gloss or baseball cards or a small toy, but the drawing adds the thrill of expectation to the event. Make sure that by the time your guests leave in the morning, everyone's name has been drawn. Another way to offer surprises is to have big bags lined up with numbers on them. Each bag introduces the next activity. For instance, one bag may be filled with pillowcases and paints for the pillow-decorating craft. Another bag may have a basketball in it as you plan to go play basketball. Using this surprise bag approach, you build the anticipation and intrigue for each new activity.

Tiring Activities. Now it is time to wear out the kids a little so they expend some of their youthful energy. I want to break this down into two possibilities. You may want to take the kids to another location to run and play and enjoy. On the other hand, you may want them to stay at your home the entire evening. Either way, it is important that you have adequate supervision for the kids.

Away-from-home possibilities include these:

- Bowling
- Laser tag
- Paintball
- Mall scavenger hunt
- Video scavenger hunt
- Roller skating
- Ice skating, hockey, or broomball
- Hayride
- Gymnastics or tumbling place
- Indoor rock climbing or obstacle course
- Gymnasium for basketball or broom hockey

- Soccer field (indoor or outdoor)
- Playground or park
- Indoor or outdoor swimming (make sure you have a lifeguard on hand)
- Sometimes churches or private schools will rent out their facilities, so check out what is available in your area.

At-home possibilities include the following:

- Outdoor games (see chapter 14)
- Tug-of-war
- Old-fashioned races: wheelbarrow, three-legged, sack
- Swimming (make sure you have a lifeguard on hand)
- Running through sprinklers
- Hide-and-seek
- Nature scavenger hunt
- Video scavenger hunt
- Basketball shoot-out game
- Movement games such as Twister
- Make your own movie

Video Scavenger Hunt. Notice that I mentioned the video scavenger hunt in both home and away possibilities. A video scavenger hunt (or it can be a photo scavenger hunt) is a wonderful slumber party idea for older kids because it allows them some freedom and creativity, plus it gives them something to come back and watch. Half the fun is in creating the video; half the fun is in watching the video and telling stories about your group's adventures. Break up into teams, give each group a list of funny things to photograph, and send them out in groups (an adult with each group). You can give point values for different photos. Photo ops include forming a human pyramid, visiting an athletic event, playing at a playground, finding items at certain stores, posing with a statue, eating a picnic, making paper hats and wearing them in a public place, doing some act of service, etc. Make sure everyone knows the importance of being courteous to others and being careful not to disrupt a place of business.

Refreshments. Provide some good snacks for the kids to enjoy after the tiring games. Chips and dip, trail mix, popcorn, and pretzels are perfect snacks. And have lots of water bottles. Remember to stay away from caffeine and limit sugar. Most root beer is caffeine free, as well as many of the lighter-colored drinks and lemonade.

Pajama Change. It is a good idea to make this a part of the schedule and not leave it up to whenever the kids feel like getting ready for bed. Designate a certain time when everyone needs to be changed into pajamas and in their bedroll. Tell them you will start the movie, but only when everyone is changed into pajamas and snuggled in their sleeping bags. You may want to consider giving out new toothbrushes and a decorated plastic cup to everyone (perhaps donated by a local dentist). Encourage everyone to go to the bathroom before they enter their sleeping bag.

Movie. All I can say is choose a good one! If you want the kids to stay put and remain interested, you need to choose a movie that they love, even if they have seen it several times. It also needs to be age-appropriate, so do your homework. You may need the input of your own child as well as that of other moms and kids. Your hope here is that the kids will lie down and listen to the movie and slowly fall asleep. Turn off the lights and encourage everyone to be quiet so all can hear the movie. You may want to say with a smile, "Whisper!" if any kids begin to talk.

Morning Light

Begin with a Sizzle. Bacon is a great way to get the kids to the kitchen. Very few people can resist the smell of bacon, so begin sizzling up a slab and you will notice guests slowly showing up in your kitchen. Scrambled eggs are generally easy for large groups and liked by most kids. But don't stop there!

Delicious Doughnuts. What slumber party is complete without doughnuts? You can certainly go out and buy some doughnuts, but it is more fun to make them at home, and the kids love it! You will need canned biscuits, oil, and powdered sugar. Use a tiny cookie cutter or knife to cut a hole in the center of each biscuit. Heat up the oil on medium. Test the heat with the holes you cut out. You don't want the doughnuts to brown too quickly. Cook the donuts in oil, lightly browning both sides. Set them out on paper towels to cool and drain. Fill a bag with powdered sugar and place doughnuts inside, shaking the bag until they are covered, or simply sprinkle the tops with powdered sugar or cinnamon sugar. Allow the kids to do the sugar part themselves. The kids will love it!

If you don't want to go the doughnut route, consider muffins or pancakes. You can purchase pancake mix in a plastic container. All you do is add water and shake. The kids love to get in on the action and pour their own pancakes if they are old enough.

You can also make fruit smoothies using your blender or yogurt parfaits layering granola, yogurt, and fruit.

Everyone begins emerging at different times, so you may want to have the early-bird risers help you with setting the table or even making the doughnuts or pancakes.

Morning Activity. It is a good idea to have a few morning activities up your sleeve if you sense the kids could use a little direction. A great beginning activity can be the cleanup game. Tell everyone to gather around the room where the sleeping bags are laid out. Tell them you want to see if it is possible to get their sleeping bags rolled up and by the front door within two minutes. Ready, go! Time them and count down the last fifteen seconds. They will love the challenge. Give them a prize if you feel like it, but most kids just enjoy the challenge and victory of racing against the clock and winning. You may also want to add challenges for getting dressed, collecting their things, and gathering trash.

If you have girls, you may want to consider some of the following morning ideas:

- *Makeovers.* Have a makeup rep join you to do facials and makeovers.
- *Manicures and Pedicures.* Set out an assortment of nail polish and designate an area in the house (you may want to cover the carpet!) for the girls to paint one another's nails.
- *Scrapbooks.* Purchase small scrapbooks that the girls can decorate with stickers and markers. Print out pictures from the night before, and give them a few to put in their scrapbooks as a memory of the event. Be sure to take at least one group picture so the girls can have a copy.
- *Plastic Frames.* Along the same lines, provide simple plastic frames, and allow the girls to decorate with appliqués, stickers, and jewels. Give them a group picture to put in the frame.

If you have boys, consider some of the following morning activities:

- *Treasure Hunt.* Provide clues that they must follow to discover a treasure box filled with their favor bags, or allow them to find the favors along the hunt.
- *Free Play in the Backyard.* Sometimes boys just need to run and play with no structure. If you have an inviting backyard, allow them to play until the parents arrive.

- *Animal Safari.* Hide animal figures (stuffed or plastic) throughout your house or yard. Tell the boys they must find three animals before they return to base camp (the kitchen). The first one to find three wins a prize.
- *Tennis Ball Team Relay.* You need at least six players and two tennis balls for this race. Break into two teams. Let the teams choose team names. Determine a start and a finish line about one hundred yards apart. (You can make the course longer for older kids.) The course can wind around and go up and down hills. The two teams line up at the starting line in two single-file lines. At the command "Go!" the first person in line gives the tennis ball a kick and then runs to the back of the line so the second player can give a kick. Each player, after kicking the tennis ball, runs to the back of the line, allowing the next player to kick. The first team to get its tennis ball over the finish line wins.

As parents pick up their kids, greet them at the door and thank them for allowing their child to visit. All's well that ends well, so be sure to end on an upbeat note and with a smile (and then go crash for the rest of the day). You may want to close with the following devotional, or use it as a family devotional. Either way, enjoy the blessed opportunity to show hospitality to the precious ones who visit your home.

Family Fun Devotional

Read: Psalm 4:8 (for older kids, read all of Psalm 4)

Talk:

- Why does the psalmist say he can lie down in peace and sleep?
- Do you feel at peace when you go to sleep at night?
- How can you enjoy the peace God's presence brings?

Do:

Make family pillowcases. Give each member of your family a new pillowcase and some paints or permanent markers. You will need to put paper or a paper grocery sack in the pillow to prevent the paint from leaking through. Ask everyone to put three things on their pillowcase: their name, Psalm 4:8 (written out), and a picture that shows something about their personality or interests. You may need to assist the younger ones as they create their pillowcases. Show and tell about your creations to the rest of the family.

Serendipity

There is one thing which gives radiance to everything.
It is the idea of something around the corner.

G. K. CHESTERTON

The hopes of the godly result in happiness, but the expectations of the wicked are all in vain.

PROVERBS 10:28 NLT

Are you familiar with the word *serendipity?* You may have heard of it as the title of a Hollywood movie or the name of a fancy dessert shop in New York City. The term was coined by Horace Walpole in his tale *The Three Princes of Serendip*, who apparently had an aptitude for making fortunate discoveries accidentally. *Serendipity* has come to mean an unexpected and wonderful experience or blessing.

We may be surprised by an unexpected blessing, but it is no surprise to God! I believe he plans little serendipities all around us—blessings waiting to be discovered. Scripture tells us that he is the giver of good gifts. It is wonderful to experience precious blessings from the hand of God and recognize his work in our lives. It also brings us great joy to give thanks to him for the way he takes care of us.

Have you ever thought about asking God to bless your family time together? My friend Caroline asks God to bless each and every family trip they take. She asks him to bless the trips in unexpected ways, and she has seen his faithful hand each time. I want Caroline to tell you her story.

A Whale of a Tale

I just knew this was going to be a trip of a lifetime! A family vacation in Hawaii! We'd be celebrating our oldest daughter's thirteenth birthday while we were there, officially ushering us all into a new teen era. My heart was bursting with excitement!

From the moment I started making our travel plans, I began to pray and turn every detail over to God, asking him to be our Travel Guide. As the trip grew closer, I prayed the Lord would bless our vacation with family fun, lasting memories, and even more, that we would sense his presence as we enjoyed the beauty of his creation.

God answered in amazing ways, one weighing in at nearly forty tons! After settling into our hotel, I visited the concierge to make reservations for a few island activities. Brochures on whale watching caught my eye, and I asked to book a short afternoon expedition. The concierge discouraged my choice, telling me we'd hit the end of the whale's calving season. Most of them had already begun to migrate back to Alaska for the northern summer. The last couple of outings resulted in very few, if any, whale sightings. I decided to book the cruise anyway. If we didn't see any whales, we would all still enjoy being out on the aqua-blue water.

As we boarded the large catamaran, our guide informed us whale sightings had been few and far between. Their radios were listening for areas of whale activity reported from other boats. Within twenty minutes, the captain came over the loudspeaker announcing a pod had been spotted and we were heading that direction.

What we saw was awesome! A huge pod of about fourteen

whales was playing and breeching out of the water. The boat's crew seemed as surprised and excited by the sight as any of us. In fact, the captain told us he hadn't seen a pod this big the entire season. From the deck, we watched those majestic humpbacks with complete awe. Some were as big as forty-five feet long. One hour and two rolls of film later, it was time for us to head back to shore.

The harbor in sight, our boat slowed to an unexpected stop. A female humpback and her baby calf were actively playing in the waters ahead. They had come too close to the boat for us to continue. What a sight! With her nose, the mother whale pushed her calf as they passed alongside us. We watched them and waited until they were safely in the distance.

My heart was pounding with praise as we docked at the harbor. The words of Psalm 104 came to my mind:

> How many are your works, O Lord!
>   In wisdom you made them all;
>   the earth is full of your creatures.
> There is the sea, vast and spacious,
>   teeming with creatures beyond number—
>   living things both large and small. (verses 24–25)

I said, "Thank you, Lord! Thank you for sending a 'providential pod' for us to experience and enjoy as a family! Your creation gives you glory! This trip is a gift from you. Thank you for your presence with us!"

We couldn't stop talking about the whales as we drove along the Maui coast in the taxi back to our hotel. Suddenly, my husband pointed out the window to the ocean. "Look! I just saw a whale jump right out of the water over there!"

Turning our heads in unison, we saw a whale fully breech out of the water. A few seconds later, out he came *again*, splashing onto his back. Wow. We were *still* seeing whales!

Our taxi driver was also impressed. Turning back toward us, she declared, "You all have good mojo!" (Webster defines *mojo* as magical power or good luck.) In fact, we had no "mojo" at all. What we had was an encore whale presentation from the King of all creation.

When it comes to family vacations, we've come to expect the unexpected. Time and time again, as we've prayed through our trips together, our family has seen the Lord answer in creative, personal ways. His blessings have come in various forms, such as upgraded hotel rooms or our favorite Dairy Queen ice cream cake delivered to our cabin by a total stranger. He's put strong knots in our family ties and given us great memories to look back on. In my heart, I know that God loves being invited on our family vacations. I'm already talking with him about next summer. . . . We're going to the Grand Canyon.[1]

Great Expectations

What are you expecting from God? As we look to him in great expectation, our eyes will be turned toward him in hope. Our perspective changes when we live with expectation. Our expectations are not necessarily that things will work out perfectly or that we will have some great, special experience, but our expectation is in the Lord. Our hope is in his presence and his work in our lives, whether things are going great or things are challenging.

May the following anonymous poem be an encouragement to us in fun times or in difficult ones. We cannot understand all God's ways, but we can trust him.

> I do not know what may befall
> Of sunshine or of rain;
> I do not know what may be mine,
> Of pleasure and of pain;

conclusion

But this I know—my Savior knows,
And whatsoe'er it be,
Still I can trust His love to give
What will be best for me.

A fun attitude begins with a heart of hope. We can hope for the best when it comes to circumstances; but more important, we can place our hope in Christ. Our hope is not in a continual fun party or a constant walk down the easy street of life. It is in the one who loves us and redeemed us. My prayer for you is that you will experience the joy of wonderful experiences with your family and friends, and more important, that you will experience the true joy that only Christ can give.

If you would like to know more about a relationship with Christ and want to speak to someone directly, please call 1-888-NEED-HIM.

Family Fun Devotional

Read: Psalm 31:14–16

Talk:

- Who holds our future?
- When is the last time you prayed for God's favor?
- Do you think the Lord wants us to pray for his blessings?

Do:

Serendipity Scrapbook

This is a book of thanksgiving, thanking the Lord for the special, unexpected blessings he has given to you and your family. You can have each family member make one. Write stories and Scriptures, and add pictures of fun adventures. Remember, a serendipity is not necessarily a perfect vacation—it can be a challenge your family went through, yet you recognized God's grace and help in the process.

Books and Resources

The most wasted of all our days are those in which we have not laughed.

SEBASTIAN CHAMFORT

Fun and Laughter

Arp, David, and Claudia Arp. *The Connected Family.* West Monroe, La.: Howard Publishing, 2005.

Babb, Martin. *When Did Caesar Become a Salad and Jeremiah a Bullfrog?* West Monroe, La.: Howard Publishing, 2005.

Callaway, Phil. *Laughing Matters: Learning to Laugh When Life Stinks.* Sisters, Ore.: Multnomah, 2005.

Davis, Ken. *Lighten Up!* Grand Rapids: Zondervan, 2000.

Johnson, Barbara. *Humor Me.* Nashville: W Publishing, 2003.

———. *Laughter from Heaven.* Nashville: W Publishing Group, 2004.

Meberg, Marilyn. *Choosing the Amusing.* Nashville: W Publishing, 1999.

Phillips, Bob. *The Awesome Book of Heavenly Humor.* Eugene, Ore.: Harvest House, 2003.

Phillips, Bob, and Steve Russo. *Jammin' Jokes for Kids.* Eugene, Ore.: Harvest House, 2004.

Save, Vickie. *Kids' Bible Activities.* Uhrichsville, Ohio: Barbour, 2005.

Streiker, Lowell D., comp. *Nelson's Big Book of Laughter.* Nashville: Thomas Nelson, 2000.

Uncle John's Book of Fun. Ashland, Ore.: Bathroom Reader's Institute, 2004.

Discipline

Campbell, Ross, M.D. *How to Really Parent Your Child.* Nashville: W Publishing, 2005.

Lehman, Kevin. *Making Children Mind Without Losing Yours.* Grand Rapids: Revell, 2000.

Tripp, Tedd. *Shepherding a Child's Heart.* Wapwallopen, Pa.: Shepherd Press, 1995.

Moral Values and Character Qualities

Bennett, William J. *Moral Compass.* New York: Simon & Schuster, 1995.

———. *The Book of Virtues.* New York: Simon & Schuster, 1993.

Hermie and Friends books and videos. Nashville: Tommy Nelson.
VeggieTales videos. www.bigidea.com.

Conversation Starters

Ladd, Karol. *Table Talk: Conversation Starters Around the Dinner Table.*
Nashville: Broadman & Holman, 2000.

Laur, Maureen, and Julie Pfitzinger. *Keep Talking: Daily Conversation Starters
for the Family Meal.* Liguori, Mo.: Liguori Publications, 2005.

Poole, Garry. *Complete Book of Questions: 1001 Conversation Starters for Any
Occasion.* Grand Rapids: Zondervan, 2003.

Smith, Julienne. *Food for Talk: Bringing Families Together One Conversation at a
Time.* New York: Running Press, 2006.

Ideas

Krueger, Caryl Waller. *1001 Things to Do with Your Kids.* Nashville: Abingdon
Press, 1998.

Wise, Debra. *Great Big Book of Children's Games.* New York: McGraw-Hill,
2003.

Recipes

Byrn, Anne. *The Cake Mix Doctor.* New York: Workman Publishing, 1999.

Wilson, Mimi, and Mary Beth Lagerborg. *Once-a-Month Cooking.* Colorado
Springs: Focus on the Family, 1999.

————. *Table Talk: Easy Activity and Recipe Ideas for Bringing Your Family
Closer at Mealtime.* Colorado Springs: Focus on the Family, 1994.

Church cookbooks! Just about every church has created one at one time.
Typically they are the most practical and best-tasting recipes.

Gaither, Gloria, and Shirley Dobson. *Creating Family Traditions.* Sisters, Ore.:
Multnomah, 2004.

————. *Making Ordinary Days Extraordinary!* Sisters, Ore.: Multnomah, 2004.

Germany, Rebecca, and Kelly Williams. *In the Kitchen with Mary and Martha.*
Uhrichsville, Ohio: Barbour, 2005.

Hall, Dawn. Busy People's cookbooks. Nashville: Rutledge Hill Press.

A laugh is a smile that bursts.

MARY WALDRIP

Notes

Chapter 1—Laughter: The Perfect Glue for Family Bonding

1. Donald O. Bolander, comp., *Instant Quotation Dictionary* (New York: Dell, 1972), 189.
2. Dr. Laurence Peter, *The Laughter Prescription* (New York: Ballantine, 1982).
3. Norman Cousins, *Anatomy of an Illness* (New York: Bantam, 1981).
4. You can read more about Lisa Whelchel's ideas by visiting her Web site: www.Momtime.com.
5. Ken Davis, *Lighten Up!* (Grand Rapids: Zondervan, 2000), 74.

Chapter 3—Being Fun

1. Used by permission from Jennifer McMahan.
2. Used by permission from Helen Howard, Coppell, Texas.

Chapter 7—Terrific Travel Tips

1. Used by permission from Karen Smith.

Chapter 8—Keeping Your Sanity While Shopping

1. Caryl Waller Krueger, *1001 Things to Do with Your Kids* (New York: Galahad Books, 1988), 73.

Chapter 9—Five Ingredients for Enjoying a Delightful Meal

1. http://casacolumbia.org/absolutenm/articlefiles/380-2005_family_dinners_ii_final.pdf.
2. Ibid.
3. Used by permission from Sammy Young.

Chapter 13—Every Occasion Can Be a Great Occasion

1. Used by permission from LaVerne Davis.

Chapter 14—Outdoor Games and Adventures

1. Many of these game ideas came from Debra Wise, *Great Big Book of Children's Games* (New York: McGraw-Hill, 2003).

Conclusion—Serendipity

1. Used by permission from Caroline Boykin.